GENIUS
LEGO®
INVENTIONS
with Bricks
You Already Have

GENIUS LEGO® INVENTIONS

with Bricks You Already Have

40 New Robots, Vehicles, Contraptions, Gadgets, Games and Other Fun STEM Creations

SARAH DEES

author of *Awesome LEGO® Creations with Bricks You Already Have*
and *Epic LEGO® Adventures with Bricks You Already Have*,
founder of Frugal Fun for Boys and Girls

PAGE STREET
PUBLISHING CO.

PAGE STREET
PUBLISHING CO.

First published in 2018 by

Page Street Publishing Co.

27 Congress Street, Suite 105

Salem, MA 01970

www.pagestreetpublishing.com

Distributed by Macmillan, sales in Canada by The Canadian Manda Group.

22   21 20 19 18   1 2 3 4 5

ISBN-13: 978-1-62414-678-7

ISBN-10: 1-62414-678-3

Library of Congress Control Number: 2018950253

Cover and book design by Meg Baskis for Page Street Publishing Co.

Photography by Sarah Dees

Printed and bound in the United States

DEDICATION

To Jordan and our LEGO-loving kids—Aidan, Gresham, Owen, Jonathan and Janie. Creating this book with you all was an amazing adventure!

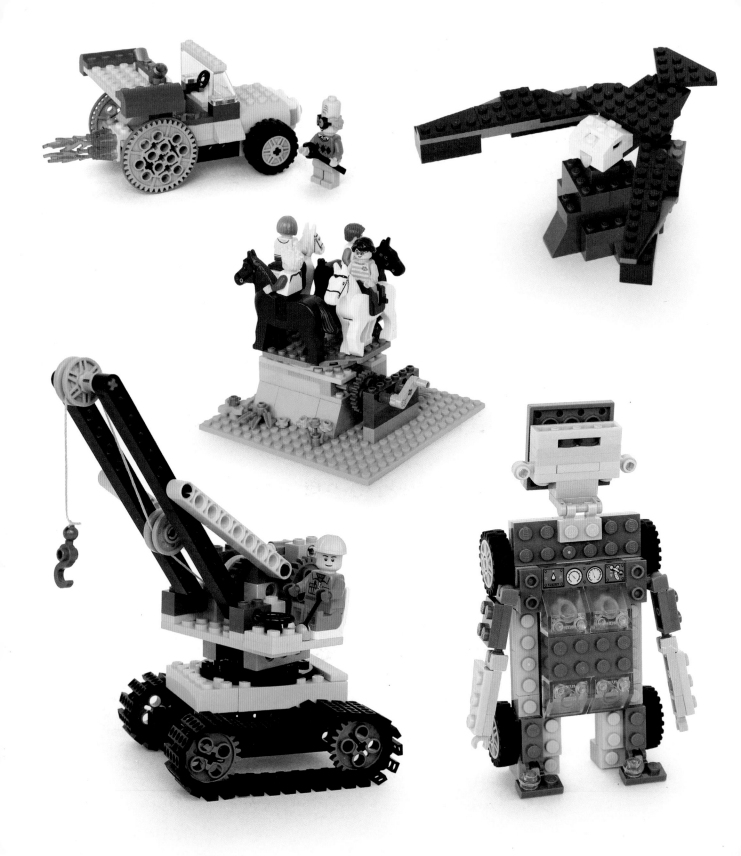

CONTENTS

HOW TO USE THIS BOOK

CALLING ALL INVENTORS!

Are you an inventor? Do you like to build and create things? Do you enjoy tinkering and figuring out how things work? Well, that's perfect, because building with LEGO bricks is all about inventing and being creative. Doing creative things is important work because it makes the world a much more interesting place. The next time you look at a painting or gaze at a city skyline or play a new board game or savor a delicious meal, you are enjoying the results of someone's creativity.

Now, you might not feel very creative, but everyone can be creative. It just takes some practice. Just like a runner trains for a marathon by exercising to build his or her strength, creativity is a muscle that needs to be exercised. Whenever you build or design something, you become better at building and designing. Thinking of new ideas leads to thinking of even more new ideas—and your ideas start to become amazing!

This book is full of really genius LEGO inventions to create with your bricks. In fact, you will be amazed at all the things your LEGO bricks can do! Consider this book to be a training manual that will launch you on your own inventing journey. The projects in this book have step-by-step instructions because it can be challenging to figure out how to build something without seeing exactly which bricks were used to build it. You'll probably be able to follow the instructions just by looking at the pictures, but each step has written instructions as well, in case you need them.

The instructions in this book are there to help you, but really the main point of this book is to inspire you to create your own inventions. Don't feel like you have to build a project exactly as it's shown in the pictures! Substitute other colors or types of bricks if you don't have the bricks shown. You may discover a modification that makes an invention even better! Most of the projects in this book, such as the robots, the 3-D Marble Maze Cube (page 177) and the Long-Distance Race Car (page 115) can easily be adapted with whichever bricks you have on hand.

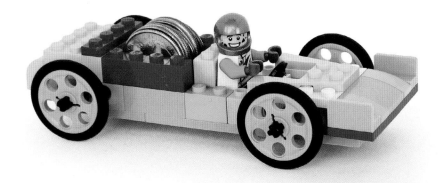

ORDERING INDIVIDUAL BRICKS

In addition to instructions, each project also begins with a parts list of all the bricks you'll need. Use the parts list to organize your bricks ahead of time or to order any pieces you don't have.

As I mentioned before, the parts list is not a set of rules! Feel free to modify the projects however you want. You will probably find a project or two, however, that you really want to build just like it's shown, but you don't have all the bricks you need. It's easy to order just the pieces you want. One option is to order through the Pick-A-Brick section on Lego.com. Each LEGO brick has a very tiny ID number, usually located on the bottom of the brick. These numbers can be hard to see, but once you find the ID number, you can enter it on Lego.com and find the exact element you need. Note that the ID number is specific to the brick shape only, not the color.

Another great option for ordering individual LEGO bricks is to visit bricklink.com. Brick Link is a site that hosts many different sellers of LEGO bricks. You can buy individual bricks, both new and used, as well as minifigures and new or retired sets. The prices on Brick Link are related to supply and demand, so you'll pay a lower price for a basic brick in a common color than you will for a rare collectible minifigure. Keep in mind that each seller on Brick Link charges separately for shipping, so you'll want to find one seller that has several different things you need. You don't want to order 5 bricks from 5 different vendors and pay a separate shipping fee each time!

LEGO bricks come in many different colors. The colors are listed on the Pick-A-Brick section of LEGO.com, and the Brick Link site also has a color guide. Because Brick Link vendors sell both new and used bricks, they have a color system that includes names for older colors that have now been discontinued. The Brick Link color system is used in this book, but do note that the current light gray and dark gray bricks are actually referred to as light bluish gray and dark bluish gray on Brick Link.

Be sure to get permission from Mom or Dad before making any purchases, and get their help when using websites such as Brick Link and the official LEGO site!

BONUS ONLINE MATERIAL!

For video demonstrations of all the projects in this book, visit frugalfun4boys.com/genius-lego-inventions.

BRICK GUIDE

You may not be aware of this, but LEGO bricks have names. If you're building a set that you purchased, it's not necessary to know what the bricks are called. However, if you're wanting to order a few individual bricks online, it will be hard to track them down without some idea of their names. And wow—there are many, many different LEGO bricks and pieces to choose from! This brick guide is not a complete list of LEGO bricks, but it will help you understand the terms used in the parts lists and track down bricks that you want to order online.

Remember that LEGO bricks have a tiny ID number printed on them. You may have to hold the brick in the right light to see it because they are very tiny! You can enter the ID number on the Pick-A-Brick or Bricks & Pieces sections of LEGO.com. Bricks & Pieces is located under customer service on the LEGO site, and you can find any LEGO element there using the ID number. Pick-A-Brick is designed to make it easy to order the most common LEGO bricks, while Bricks & Pieces is more comprehensive.

If you're using Brick Link, the names of bricks will vary slightly from the names used on LEGO.com. This book uses the Brick Link naming system.

A NOTE ABOUT TECHNIC BRICKS

On the next few pages, you'll find a brick guide and some tips that will help you with building LEGO inventions. One thing to note is that many of the bricks that are labeled "Technic bricks" come in more sets than just Technic sets. Many other types of sets contain the Technic elements that are needed for the projects in this book, so you'll want to check your LEGO collection before ordering Technic pieces. You may have them after all!

BRICKS

These are bricks. Count the number of dots (studs) to determine the brick's size. For example, the dark gray brick is a 2 x 4 and the yellow brick is a 1 x 6.

MODIFIED BRICKS

Bricks that have been changed in some way are called "bricks, special" on Pick-A-Brick and "bricks, modified" on Brick Link. Bricks can be modified with studs on the side, clips, handles, pins and more. The yellow brick is a 1 x 1 brick with one stud on the side. Some of the bricks of this type also have a little notch below the stud. Those types of bricks are referred to as headlights.

ROUND BRICKS

The brown brick is a 4 x 4 round brick. The red brick is a 2 x 2 rounded corner brick. Round bricks are used throughout this book.

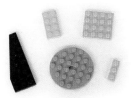

PLATES

Flat bricks are called plates by both Brick Link and Pick-A-Brick. There are plates, such as the 4 x 4 tan plate shown, as well as round plates and wedge plates. Some wedge plates have either a right or left orientation. The dark blue brick is a 3 x 8 wedge plate, left.

MODIFIED PLATES

Like bricks, plates can also be modified with a socket, a handle, a clip, a tooth and so on. This book especially uses plates that have an added pin hole, such as the dark gray 1 x 2 plate with a pin hole on top. Brick Link refers to these plates as "plates, modified" and Pick-A-Brick calls them "plates, special."

SLOPE BRICKS

These types of bricks are called "slopes" on Brick Link and "roof tiles" on Pick-A-Brick. The blue brick is a 2 x 3 slope, and the lime green brick is a 1 x 3 curved slope. Bricks that slope the opposite way are called inverted. The orange brick is a 2 x 2 inverted slope.

BRACKETS

Brackets are very useful for adding studs to another side of your creation. Brick Link refers to them as brackets, while Pick-A-Brick calls them "angle plates." Both sites refer to the size of a bracket in two directions. For example, the light gray bracket is a 1 x 2—1 x 4. The dark gray is a 1 x 2—1 x 2 inverted bracket, as the second side goes up instead of down.

TILES

Tiles are plates that are completely smooth on top. Pick-A-Brick calls them "flat tiles" while on Brick Link they are just called tiles. Some tiles have pictures printed on them, such as computer keyboards, maps, gauges and buttons.

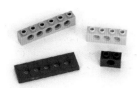

TECHNIC BRICKS AND PLATES

Bricks that have holes in them are called Technic bricks, and they are measured by counting the number of studs on top. The light gray brick is a 1 x 6 Technic brick. Technic plates are similar to regular plates, with the only difference being that they have holes.

TECHNIC LIFTARMS

Bricks with holes that are smooth without studs are called Technic liftarms on Brick Link. Pick-A-Brick refers to them as Technic beams. Liftarms are measured by the number of holes. For example, the dark gray liftarm is a 1 x 9, and the red is a 2 x 4 L-shape.

TECHNIC AXLES

Axles are very important for projects with moving parts. Technic axles are measured by how many studs long they are. The light gray axle, which is sitting next to a plate for reference, is 5 studs long. In this book, that axle will be referred to as a Technic axle, 5 studs long. The dark gray axle has a stop at the end. These are useful because you can slide them through a hole in a Technic brick and the end won't go all the way through.

PINS

Pins are essential for connecting different LEGO elements. For the most part, the color of the pin tells you how it functions. The light gray pins are smooth and allow the pieces they connect to turn freely. The black pins have friction ridges. Two bricks connected with a black pin can move, but you'll need to do the moving as they won't spin on their own. The tan pin has an axle connection on one side and a pin without friction ridges (freely spinning) on the other. The blue pin has an axle connection on one side and a pin with friction ridges on the other. Some pins are 3 studs long, such as the long blue pin. It has friction ridges, while light gray or tan pins that are 3 studs long do not have friction ridges.

TECHNIC BUSH

Technic bush are small red or light gray elements that keep pieces from moving. You can add them to axles to keep the bricks on the axles from moving side to side or sliding off.

TECHNIC GEARS

Gears are essential to creating LEGO inventions with moving parts. In the parts lists, you'll see gears referred to by the number of teeth they have. The largest gear is a 40-tooth and the one to the right of it is a 24-tooth. The top row are all spur gears, or gears with flat teeth. Below those are two light gray bevel gears. Bevel gears have rounded edges and are ideal for fitting together at a 90-degree angle. The terms "spur gears" and "bevel gears" are not specific to LEGO bricks but are used with real machines as well. The yellow gear is a knob wheel. Next to the knob wheel is a worm gear, and at the bottom of the picture is a gear rack.

CONNECTORS

There are many LEGO elements that connect axles and pins. Angled axle and pin connectors are labeled (on the actual brick) with the numbers 1 to 6. The dark gray element is a Technic connector #1. The yellow one is a Technic connector #6. The light gray brick is a Technic axle and pin connector, perpendicular, 3 studs long with a center pin hole. Wow, that's quite a mouthful! You'll need several of those to build the Ball Stairs Circuit (page 102).

SPECIAL LIFTARMS

There are a couple more liftarms worth mentioning specifically. The blue brick is a 1 x 3 thin liftarm. You can see the thick liftarm next to it for comparison. The other light gray piece is a 1 x 3 liftarm with two axle holes and a pin/crank. This brick is used several times in this book as a handle or crank.

POWER FUNCTIONS

A few of the projects in this book are powered by the LEGO M-motor and battery box. The upper battery box is designed to be attached to Technic elements, and the lower battery box can be attached to bricks with studs.

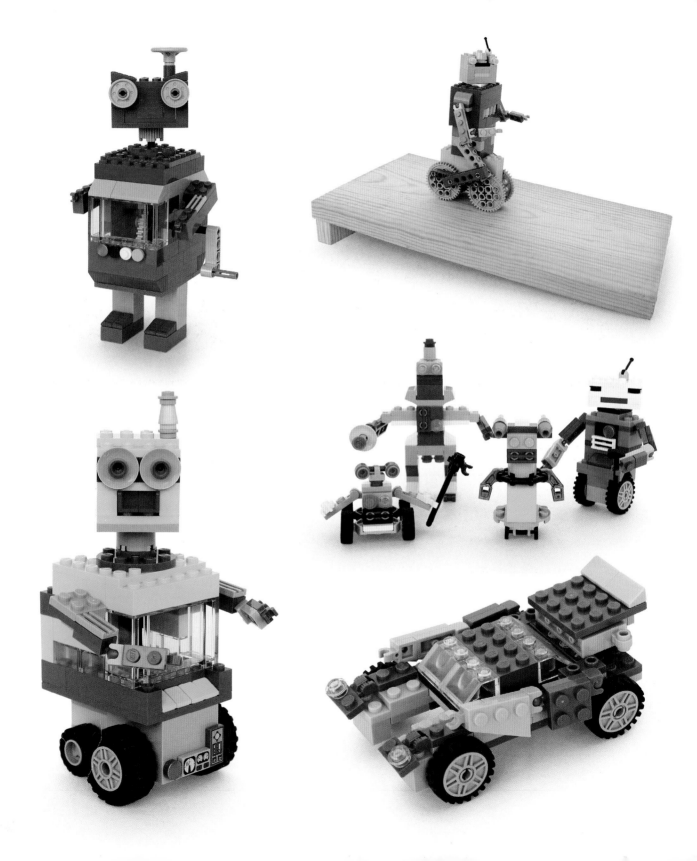

MARVELOUS MOVING ROBOTS

Robots are incredibly fascinating to people of all ages. Both young and old enjoy designing and playing with them, and today, robots are more amazing and useful than ever. Robots are used to carry out tasks in factories that would be too messy or repetitive for humans to perform. They protect humans by seeking out and detonating explosives and by investigating hazardous environments to check for substances that could harm people. Robots perform vital functions in the fields of medicine and space exploration, as well as being used in everyday life. For example, scientists are developing robots that sense motion in your home and take photos of possible intruders. They can even recognize familiar faces! What will the robots of the future be able to do? Maybe you will become an engineer and help shape the future of robotics!

With the projects in this chapter, you can create LEGO robots with mechanical moving parts. While these robots are not programmed by computers, they will let you explore principles of mechanical engineering. Build feet that pedal on their own, use gears to control head movement and even construct a robot that transforms into a car.

RYDER THE ROBOT

This zippy little robot has a clever mechanical element—give him a push and his feet pedal along! Movable leg joints and feet attached to pistons create amazing lifelike motion. While one foot moves up, the other goes down. Try letting your robot pedal his way down a ramp. The steeper the ramp, the faster he'll pedal!

HOW IT WORKS

Ryder the Robot is constructed with a cam (a wheel with an off-center axle) driving a foot. If the feet (the Technic liftarms) were attached to the center of the gears, they wouldn't move up and down at all but instead would stay in the same position relative to the axle. By attaching the feet off-center, the wheel (the gear brick) becomes a cam, causing the feet to move. Circular motion is converted to linear motion. When humans walk, the knee moves in a circle in much the same way, although the cause of the movement is contracting muscles rather than rotating wheels. Isn't it interesting that mechanical bodies have similarities to human bodies?

PARTS LIST

LIGHT GRAY BRICKS
1—2 x 2 truncated cone
2—2 x 4 plates
2—1 x 2 plates
1—2 x 8 plate
3—1 x 2 bricks
2—1 x 1 bricks
2—1 x 1 bricks with a stud on the side (headlight)
3—1 x 1 round bricks
2—1 x 4 Technic bricks
2—1 x 6 Technic bricks
2—1 x 2 plates with a socket on the end
2—1 x 2 plates with a socket on the side
2—1 x 2 plates with a clip on the end

DARK GRAY BRICKS
7—2 x 4 bricks
2—1 x 4 bricks
2—1 x 6 bricks
2—1 x 6 plates
2—4 x 6 plates
2—1 x 2 plates with a ball on the side
2—1 x 2 plates with a ball on the end
2—1 x 7 Technic liftarms
2—1 x 6 Technic bricks

GREEN BRICKS
2—2 x 4 bricks
2—2 x 3 bricks with a curved end
1—4 x 4 plate
2—1 x 4 plates

YELLOW BRICKS
1—1 x 2 plate
1—1 x 1 round brick
3—2 x 2 bricks
3—2 x 6 bricks

ASSORTED BRICKS
1—yellow lever (antenna)
2—black Technic axles, 4 studs long
2—green light cover with internal bar (LEGO ID 58176)
2—2 x 2 turntables
2—1 x 8 black Technic bricks
10—light gray Technic pins
4—Technic gears, 40 tooth

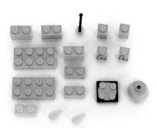

STEP 1: Gather the bricks shown for building the robot's head.

STEP 2: Attach three 1 x 2 bricks and a 1 x 2 plate to a 2 x 4 plate. The 1 x 2 plate is in the front.

STEP 3: Add a 1 x 2 yellow plate and another 1 x 2 light gray plate.

STEP 4: Attach the 2 x 2 truncated cone to the turntable. Place this on top of the robot's head. Attach the light covers to the 1 x 1 bricks with a stud on the side.

STEP 5: Place the eyes on top of the head and add a 1 x 1 brick behind each one. Add a lever to make the robot's antenna.

STEP 6: Start building the body. Grab two 2 x 4 dark gray bricks.

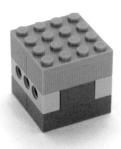

STEP 7: Add a 2 x 4 dark gray brick and two 1 x 4 light gray Technic bricks.

STEP 8: Add two 2 x 4 green bricks and a 4 x 4 green plate to the robot's body.

STEP 9: Place three more 2 x 4 dark gray bricks on top of the body.

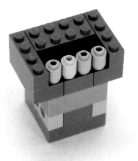

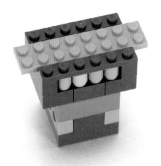

STEP 10: Add two 1 x 4 dark gray bricks and a 2 x 4 dark gray brick. Then use 1 x 1 round bricks to decorate the front of the robot's body.

STEP 11: Place two 1 x 6 dark gray plates on top of the body and add a 2 x 8 light gray plate in the middle.

STEP 12: For the shoulders, place a 1 x 2 dark gray plate with a ball on each side of the body. Then add a 4 x 6 dark gray plate.

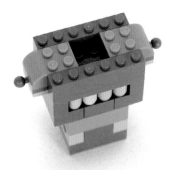

STEP 13: Add two 1 x 6 dark gray bricks and two 2 x 3 green bricks with a curved end.

STEP 14: Finish up the body with a 4 x 6 dark gray plate and a 2 x 2 turntable.

STEP 15: Attach the robot's head to the turntable. Now his head can spin!

STEP 16: Build the robot's arms. Each arm has a 1 x 4 green plate attached to a 1 x 2 light gray plate with a socket on the end and a 1 x 2 light gray plate with a socket on the side. Then add a 1 x 2 dark gray plate with a ball on the end and a 1 x 2 light gray plate with a clip on the end.

STEP 17: Attach the arms to the robot's body.

STEP 18: Now build the mechanism that makes the robot pedal. Gather the bricks shown. The black bricks are 1 x 8 Technic bricks.

STEP 19: Stack the bricks as shown.

STEP 20: Build the wheels. Find four 40-tooth Technic gears, four light gray pins and two 1 x 7 dark gray Technic liftarms.

STEP 21: Attach the liftarms to the gears. Make sure that each liftarm is attached to the equivalent hole on both gears.

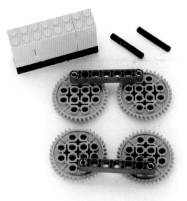

STEP 22: Grab the bricks from Step 19 and two black axles (4 studs long).

STEP 23: Attach the wheels to the base by sliding the axles through the center X-shaped axle hole on each gear. Make sure that the liftarm on one side is up while the other one is down. It's easy to move the liftarms after the gear is attached to the axle. Just pull out the pins and make adjustments if needed.

STEP 24: Build the legs. Each leg has two 1 x 6 Technic bricks and three light gray pins.

STEP 25: Attach the legs. The legs will connect to the light gray Technic bricks on the robot's body and the dark gray liftarms at the bottom. Once the legs are attached, your robot is complete!

Push your robot and watch him pedal! It's also fun to let him move on his own by putting him on a ramp. Try experimenting with the height of the ramp. How fast can Ryder the Robot pedal without tipping over?

SATELLITE THE ROBOT

Build a cute little robot with a big personality. His funny mouth will make you smile! This robot also has a fun trick to perform. Turn the knob on his back and his head rotates from side to side with the help of two gears inside his body. Build him with a clear front so that you can see the gears in action. If you don't have clear panels, substitute with windows. Or just build the front of his body with regular bricks.

HOW IT WORKS

Gears are super useful mechanical devices! They can be used to change the direction that something rotates or to change the speed of a rotating part. In this project, gears are used to change rotation on a vertical axis to rotation on a horizontal axis. Inside Satellite's body there are two gears whose teeth mesh together at 90-degree angles. When you turn the knob on his back, the vertical gear turns. The teeth of the vertical gear connect with the teeth of the horizontal gear, causing Satellite to turn his head.

PARTS LIST

MEDIUM AZURE BRICKS
1—2 x 6 brick
9—1 x 4 bricks
4—1 x 1 bricks
1—1 x 2 brick
4—1 x 2 slopes
9—2 x 4 plates
1—1 x 6 plate
3—1 x 1 slopes, 30 degree

LIGHT GRAY BRICKS
4—2 x 4 bricks
1—1 x 4 brick with four studs on the side
2—1 x 2 Technic bricks
1—1 x 4 Technic brick
2—2 x 2 round bricks
3—4 x 4 plates
1—2 x 4 plate
2—2 x 2 plates
2—1 x 4 plates

1—1 x 2 plate
1—2 x 4 plate with two pins
1—2 x 2 plate with two wheel holders
2—1 x 2 plates with a socket on the end
1—Technic bush
2—1 x 2 grills
2—1 x 1 round plates
2—2 x 2 dishes
1—1 x 2—1 x 2 bracket

DARK GRAY BRICKS
1—6 x 8 plate
3—1 x 4 plates
1—4 x 4 round plate
5—1 x 4 bricks
2—1 x 3 bricks
1—1 x 6 brick
1—1 x 2 brick
4—1 x 2 Technic bricks
2—1 x 2 plates with a clip on the end
1—2 x 2 round tile with a hole

2—1 x 2 plates with a ball on the end
2—Technic gears, 24 tooth

ASSORTED BRICKS
1—1 x 4 x 3 clear panel
2—1 x 2 x 3 clear panels
4—1 x 2 clear bricks
1—Technic axle, 8 studs long
1—Technic axle, 4 studs long
1—turntable 4 x 4 square base
2—black Technic pins
1—2 x 6 yellow plate
1—1 x 1 yellow slope, 30 degree
1—1 x 1 yellow cone
2—1 x 1 x 1 red corner panels
2—1 x 1 translucent blue round plates
1—1 x 1 round silver tile
2—1 x 2 tiles, printed with gauges
2—large wheels
2—small wheels

STEP 1: Attach two 2 x 4 medium azure plates to a 4 x 4 light gray plate.

STEP 2: Add two 1 x 4 medium azure bricks and a 1 x 2 medium azure brick. Then gather the bricks shown.

STEP 3: Attach the two red corner panels to the light gray bracket to make Satellite's mouth.

STEP 4: Attach the mouth to the underside of a 2 x 4 medium azure plate. Then attach the plate to the head.

STEP 5: Build the eyes. Attach a 1 x 1 translucent blue round plate and a 2 x 2 light gray dish to a 1 x 2 dark gray Technic brick. Make two of these.

STEP 6: Place the eyes on the front of the head and add a 1 x 4 medium azure brick right behind them.

STEP 7: Add one 2 x 4 medium azure plate on top of the eyes and stack two more behind the eyes.

STEP 8: Attach four 1 x 2 medium azure slopes to the back of the head.

STEP 9: Add one more 2 x 4 medium azure plate to the top of the head. Build an antenna for Satellite by stacking a 1 x 1 yellow cone and two 1 x 1 light gray round plates.

STEP 10: Attach a 2 x 4 light gray plate with two pins to a 2 x 6 yellow plate so that it overlaps by only two studs.

STEP 11: Attach the front wheels and add small wheels in the back. Then add a 1 x 4 dark gray plate just behind the front wheels.

STEP 12: Add two 4 x 4 light gray plates and two 1 x 4 medium azure bricks.

STEP 13: Attach three 2 x 4 light gray bricks.

STEP 14: Place a 6 x 8 dark gray plate onto the base of the robot. Then add dark gray bricks as shown. Find a 4 x 4 turntable base and four 1 x 1 slopes.

STEP 15: Attach the 4 x 4 turntable and 1 x 1 slopes as shown.

STEP 16: Add the clear panels and four 1 x 2 clear bricks to the front and sides of Satellite's body.

STEP 17: Place two 1 x 1 medium azure bricks and one 1 x 4 medium azure brick on each side of the body.

STEP 18: Add a 2 x 4 light gray brick in the center of the back. Then add a 1 x 2 dark gray Technic brick and a 1 x 3 dark gray brick on each side.

STEP 19: Gather the bricks shown.

STEP 20: Slide a 24-tooth gear onto an axle (8 studs long). Attach a 1 x 4 light gray plate to both the top and bottom of a 1 x 4 light gray Technic brick.

STEP 21: Add two 1 x 4 dark gray bricks and a 2 x 4 light gray plate to the bricks from the previous step.

STEP 22: Slide an axle (4 studs long) through the center hole of the light gray Technic brick. Attach the second 24-tooth gear and add a Technic bush on the other side to hold it in place.

STEP 23: Set the first gear in place inside the robot. Attach the 2 x 2 round brick to the end of the Technic axle (4 studs long).

STEP 24: Attach the gear assembly. Check to make sure that the gear teeth align correctly with each other.

STEP 25: Add a 1 x 4 medium azure brick and a 2 x 4 medium azure plate on each side.

STEP 26: Place a 2 x 6 brick and a 1 x 6 plate on the front of the robot. Then gather the bricks shown.

STEP 27: Attach the 4 x 4 round plate and the 2 x 2 tile with a hole. This will secure the axle (8 studs long) in place. Then add a 2 x 2 round brick to the underside of the head.

STEP 28: Attach Satellite's head to the top of the axle (8 studs long).

STEP 29: Gather the bricks shown. You'll need two sets of these—one for each arm.

STEP 30: Place a 2 x 2 light gray plate on top of a 1 x 4 dark gray plate and a 1 x 2 light gray Technic brick. Then add a 1 x 2 grill and attach a black pin to the Technic brick.

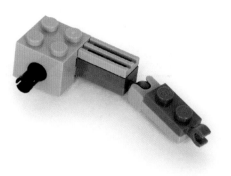

STEP 31: Turn the arm upside down and add a 1 x 2 light gray plate and a 1 x 2 dark gray plate with a ball on the end.

STEP 32: Complete the arm with a 1 x 2 plate with a socket on the end and a 1 x 2 plate with a clip on the end. Then build the second arm.

STEP 33: Attach the arms by inserting the pins into the Technic bricks on the sides of Satellite's body. Then gather the bricks shown.

STEP 34: Place the 1 x 4 brick with four studs on the side under the front of Satellite's body. Then add tiles with buttons and gauges.

Your robot is complete! Try turning his head with the knob. The moving head really makes him come to life! Pretend that he is communicating with the other robots or planning a mission to explore outer space. His hands can hold tools or other accessories.

TURBO THE TRANSFORMING ROBOT

Use your bricks to create a robot that transforms into a car, then back to a robot again! The spoiler on the back of the car unfolds to reveal the robot's head. Unfold the arms and flip up the headlights to create feet. Then your robot will stand on his own!

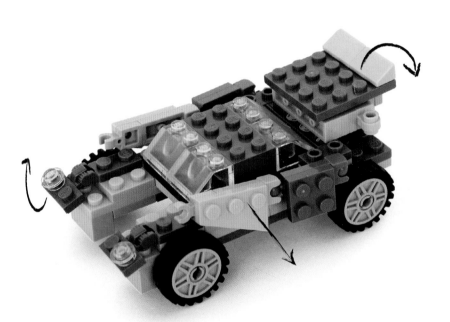

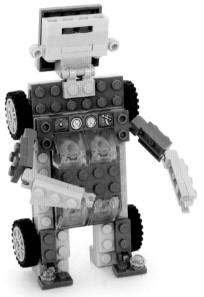

HOW IT WORKS

When engineers are designing machines, they must create moving parts that have the correct angle of rotation. Think about a living room recliner. The joints in the chair's mechanism must move (and stop moving) at certain angles for the chair to be comfortable to sit in. You wouldn't want it to be flat like a bed! Turbo's head needs to rotate nearly 180 degrees in order for it to look like both a car and a robot. By using a plate with a handle and a plate with clips as your joint, you can create an almost 180-degree rotation.

Turbo's arms use ball and socket joints. This type of joint can rotate on more than one plane. That means that the joint can rotate up and down and also side to side.

DID YOU KNOW?

Your hip and shoulder joints are ball and socket joints, similar to the joints in Turbo's arms! Can you imagine what it would be like if you could only move your shoulder in one direction? There would be so many things you couldn't do, like reach back to buckle your seatbelt or swing from the monkey bars. Our bodies have a really fantastic design!

PARTS LIST

DARK GRAY BRICKS
1—4 x 4 plate
3—2 x 6 plates
5—2 x 2 plates
1—2 x 4 brick
1—1 x 4 brick with four studs on the side
2—1 x 2 plates with a ball on the side
2—1 x 2 plates with a ball and socket on the ends
2—1 x 2 hinge plates with two fingers on the end
2—1 x 2 hinge plates with one finger on the end
1—1 x 4 tile, printed with gauges

LIGHT GRAY BRICKS
2—1 x 2 bricks
2—2 x 2 plates with a pin hole on the bottom
2—1 x 2 plates with a socket on the end
1—1 x 2 plate
4—Technic pins
1—1 x 2—1 x 2 bracket
1—1 x 2 plate with a handle on the side
1—1 x 2 plate with two clips on the side
2—1 x 1 plates with a clip

LIME GREEN BRICKS
4—2 x 6 plates
2—2 x 4 plates
4—1 x 4 plates
1—1 x 6 plate
2—2 x 2 plates

2—1 x 2 plates
2—1 x 2 slopes, 30 degree
2—1 x 1 plates
1—2 x 3 wedge plate, right
1—2 x 3 wedge plate, left
2—1 x 1 plates with a clip light

ASSORTED BRICKS
4—2 x 2 clear slopes
1—4 x 6 dark blue plate
1—1 x 4 dark blue plate
4—wheels
2—1 x 1 translucent red round plates
2—1 x 1 red round plates
1—1 x 2 white tile
2—1 x 1 translucent yellow round plates
1—1 x 2 light blue plate

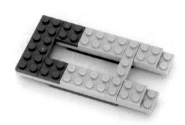

STEP 1: Grab two 2 x 6 dark gray plates.

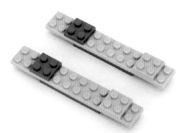

STEP 2: Place two 2 x 6 lime green plates on top of each one. Then add a 2 x 2 lime green plate and a 2 x 2 dark gray plate to each one as shown.

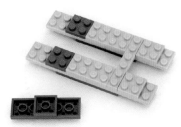

STEP 3: Connect the two sections by attaching a 1 x 6 lime green plate. Then attach a 2 x 2 dark gray plate to the center of the underside of a 2 x 6 dark gray plate.

STEP 4: Attach the dark gray plates to the body as shown.

STEP 5: Add a 4 x 6 dark blue plate and a 1 x 4 dark blue plate to the body of the robot. Then gather the bricks shown.

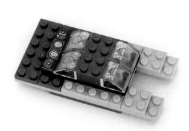

STEP 6: Place four 2 x 2 clear slopes and a 2 x 4 dark gray brick on the center of the body. Then add a 1 x 4 tile printed with gauges. If you don't have the exact brick shown, substitute another type of decorated tile.

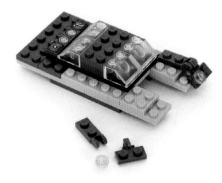

STEP 7: Make the headlights by connecting a 1 x 2 plate with two locking fingers and a 1 x 2 plate with one locking finger on the side. Then add a 1 x 1 translucent yellow round plate. These bricks can move like a hinge but will lock in place in whichever position you leave them.

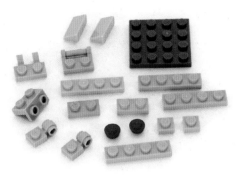

STEP 8: Gather the bricks shown for building the robot's head.

STEP 9: The robot's head will be built with the studs facing downward. Start by stacking a 1 x 4 lime green plate on top of a 1 x 2 light gray plate. Then add a 1 x 2 light blue plate and two 1 x 1 lime green plates with a clip light.

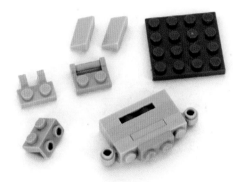

STEP 10: Add two more 1 x 4 lime green plates, and then add the red 1 x 1 round plates as the eyes. Attach two 1 x 1 lime green plates and the final 1 x 4 lime green plate on top.

STEP 11: Attach the 1 x 2 plate with clips to the 1 x 2 plate with a handle on the side. Then attach the 1 x 2—1 x 2 bracket to the underside of the 4 x 4 dark gray plate. Add two 1 x 2 lime green slopes to create a spoiler for the car.

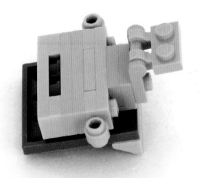

STEP 12: Connect the head to the 1 x 2 plate with a handle on the side.

STEP 13: Attach the head to the body of the robot.

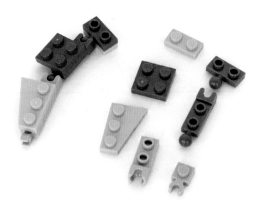

STEP 14: Gather the bricks shown for building the robot's arms.

STEP 15: Connect the arm joints as shown.

STEP 16: Add a 2 x 2 dark gray plate and a 2 x 3 lime green wedge plate.

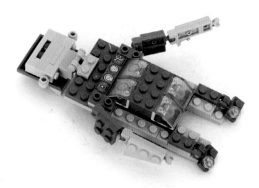

STEP 17: Attach the arms to the body right next to the 1 x 4 tile printed with gauges.

STEP 18: Turn the robot upside down and add the wheels. The wheels in the picture are attached to a 2 x 2 plate with a pinhole underneath. Use wheels like this, or substitute a different type.

STEP 19: Gather the bricks shown.

STEP 20: Attach the 1 x 2 white tile and the 1 x 1 translucent red round plates to the 1 x 4 brick with four studs on the side. Add the two 1 x 2 light gray bricks just in front of the robot's front wheels.

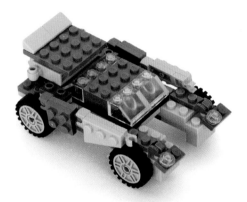

Your robot is now complete! Turn it back over and it should look like this.

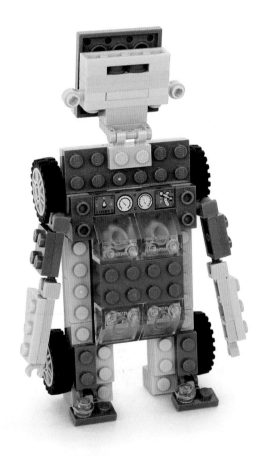

To transform your robot, first flip up the head. Then, bend the headlights upward to make the feet.

Unfold the robot's arms from the sides of his body. He should now be able to stand on his own, like this. The ball and socket joints in his arms make him very posable.

EMMA THE ROBOT

When you push Emma the Robot, her arms move up and down on their own. Emma works in a similar way to Ryder (page 16), but the motion of the gears is transferred to her arms rather than her feet. You can align the arms so that they move in sync with each other, or make one go up while the other goes down. Either way, you'll have a blast creating this mechanical toy!

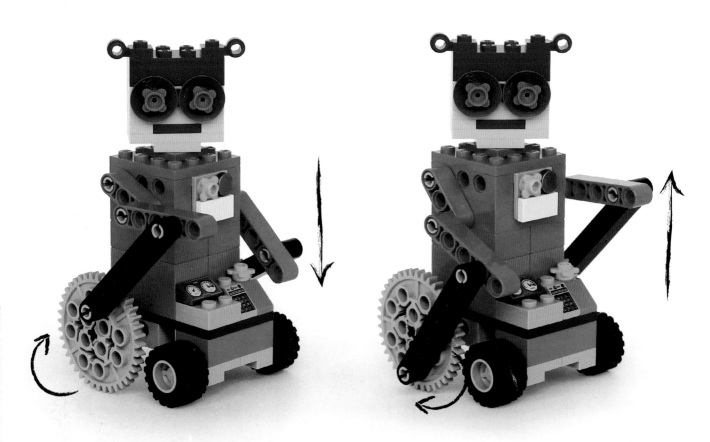

HOW IT WORKS

The mechanism in this robot is referred to as a crank. Circular motion is converted to up-and-down motion through the use of rods that are attached to the outer edge of Emma's wheels (the 40-tooth gears). As the wheels turn, they are providing energy to the rods, and the rods push Emma's arms up and then bring them down again. This same type of motion is also used in the Medieval Knight Duel on page 157.

PARTS LIST

BLUE BRICKS
5—2 x 4 bricks
1—2 x 3 brick
1—4 x 4 plate
2—1 x 2 plates
2—1 x 4 Technic bricks
2—1 x 5 Technic liftarms
2—1 x 3 Technic liftarms
1—2 x 2 turntable

LIGHT GRAY BRICKS
2—2 x 2 plates
1—1 x 2—2 x 2 bracket

1—1 x 2 slope, printed with buttons
2—Technic bushes
8—Technic pins
2—2 x 2 plates with a wheel holder
2—Technic gears, 40 tooth

TAN BRICKS
2—2 x 4 plates
1—2 x 2 plate
3—1 x 2 plates
3—1 x 4 Technic bricks

ASSORTED BRICKS
1—4 x 6 brown plate
2—1 x 7 black Technic liftarms

1—black Technic axle, 8 studs long
4—2 x 4 lavender bricks
1—1 x 2 lavender slope
1—1 x 2 purple plate
3—1 x 4 magenta bricks
2—1 x 1 magenta plates with a clip light
2—2 x 2 dark gray dishes
1—1 x 1 dark gray round tile
1—1 x 2 white tile
1—1 x 2 slope, printed with dials
2—wheels
2—pink flowers
1—light orange flower
1—green flower

STEP 1: Gather the bricks shown for building Emma's head.

STEP 2: Place three 1 x 2 tan plates and a 1 x 2 purple plate on top of a 2 x 4 tan plate.

STEP 3: Place another 2 x 4 tan plate on top. Then add a 1 x 4 tan Technic brick and a 1 x 4 magenta brick. Substitute another color for Emma's hair if you don't have magenta. Attach a flower to each of the 2 x 2 dark gray dishes to make her eyes.

STEP 4: Attach the stud on the back of each dish to the Technic brick in Emma's head. Add two more 1 x 4 magenta bricks to the top of her head, and add the 1 x 1 magenta plates with a clip light to look like hair. Place a 2 x 2 tan plate under her head.

STEP 5: Start building Emma's body by attaching two 1 x 4 tan Technic bricks and a 2 x 4 blue brick to the underside of a 4 x 6 brown plate.

STEP 6: Place the wheels under the blue brick. Then find two 40-tooth gears, a black axle (8 studs long) and two Technic bushes.

STEP 7: Slide the axle through both tan Technic bricks, and then add a Technic bush on each side to hold it in place.

STEP 8: Attach the gears to the axle using the center X-shaped axle hole.

STEP 9: Build up Emma's body with four 2 x 4 lavender bricks.

STEP 10: Add four 2 x 4 blue bricks to the body. Place two 1 x 4 blue Technic bricks and a 2 x 3 blue brick on top. Then gather the bricks shown.

STEP 11: Stack two 1 x 2 blue plates and place them at the front of the body. Attach a 1 x 2 white tile, a light orange flower and a 1 x 1 dark gray round tile to a 1 x 2—2 x 2 bracket. If you don't have these, substitute other tiles to create buttons on Emma's body.

STEP 12: Attach the bracket to Emma's body.

STEP 13: Build the arms with liftarms and light gray pins that will allow the joints to move freely. Each arm is made up of a blue 1 x 3 liftarm, a blue 1 x 5 liftarm, a black 1 x 7 liftarm and four light gray pins. Make sure that the arms are mirror images of each other.

STEP 14: Attach the arms to the hole in the Technic brick closest to Emma's back. Then connect the pin at the bottom to the 40-tooth gear.

STEP 15: Place a 4 x 4 blue plate on top of Emma's body, and then add a 2 x 2 turntable. Gather the bricks shown.

STEP 16: Stack the two 2 x 2 light gray plates and place them on the front of the body. Add the lavender slope brick and the slope bricks printed with dials and buttons, and your robot is complete!

Now check the arm function. If you want Emma's arms to move opposite from each other (one up while the other is down), make sure that the black liftarms are attached to opposite holes on the 40-tooth gears. If you want them to move in unison, attach the black liftarms to the corresponding hole on each gear.

RADIO THE ROBOT

This classic-looking robot has a funny trick to perform! Turn the handle on the side of his body and his head moves up and down. Get creative with the bricks you use on this robot. For example, his eyes are made from wheels!

HOW IT WORKS

If the gear inside Radio's body were centered on the axle, his head would simply stay at the same height as the gear turned beneath it. By placing the gear off-center on the axle, you are creating a cam (just like with Ryder [page 16]). In this machine, the cam moves a follower (the axle that holds Radio's head) by bumping it up and down as it turns.

DID YOU KNOW?

The first industrial robot, named Unimate, took its place on the General Motors car assembly line in New Jersey in 1961. The robot was invented by George Devol, and its job was to handle hot metal parts so that workers would not have to complete this dangerous task. Devol's invention improved the operations of assembly lines around the world. Unimate even made an appearance on *The Tonight Show with Johnny Carson* in 1966!

PARTS LIST

DARK GRAY BRICKS
1—6 x 6 plate
3—4 x 6 plates
3—2 x 6 plates
11—1 x 6 bricks
10—1 x 4 bricks
4—1 x 3 bricks
4—2 x 4 bricks
4—1 x 2 bricks
1—1 x 4 brick with four studs on the side
2—1 x 1 bricks
4—1 x 2 plates
4—2 x 2 plates
2—1 x 2 Technic bricks
2—1 x 2 Technic bricks with axle holes
1—1 x 1 round brick
1—1 x 1 round tile
2—1 x 2 plates with a clip on the end

LIGHT GRAY BRICKS
2—1 x 4 Technic bricks
2—1 x 4 bricks
6—2 x 2 bricks
2—1 x 2 bricks
2—2 x 4 slopes
2—2 x 2 slopes
1—2 x 4 plate
2—2 x 2 round bricks with ridges
2—1 x 2 grills
1—Technic gear, 40 tooth
2—Technic bushes
2—wheels with pin holes
1—2 x 4 L-shaped Technic liftarm, thick
1—1 x 1 round tile

RED BRICKS
2—1 x 6 bricks
3—1 x 4 bricks
4—1 x 2 bricks
2—1 x 6 Technic bricks

6—2 x 2 inverted slopes
2—2 x 2 plates (or one 2 x 4 plate)
2—1 x 2 plates
6—1 x 2 slopes with four slots
2—1 x 2 x 1 panels
1—4 x 4 round plate

ASSORTED BRICKS
1—black Technic axle, 10 studs long
1—black Technic axle, 6 studs long
1—1 x 4 x 3 panel, clear
2—1 x 2 x 3 panels, clear
1—blue Technic pin with friction ridges, 3 studs long
2—black Technic pins
2—blue Technic axle pins with friction ridges
2—1 x 2 dark tan tiles
1—1 x 1 white round plate
1—1 x 1 translucent red round tile
1—Technic steering wheel, 3 studs in diameter

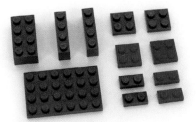

STEP 1: Gather the bricks shown for building the robot's mouth.

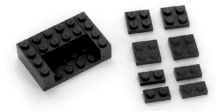

STEP 2: Attach a 2 x 4 brick and two 1 x 4 bricks to the 4 x 6 plate as shown.

STEP 3: Add two 2 x 2 red plates. Or use a 2 x 4 red plate.

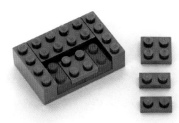

STEP 4: Make the corners of his mouth turn up by adding two 1 x 2 red plates and a 2 x 2 dark gray plate.

STEP 5: Fill in the remaining dark gray plates.

STEP 6: Gather the bricks shown for building the rest of Radio's head.

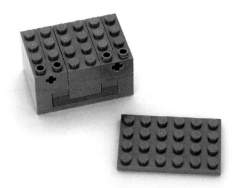

STEP 7: Attach a 4 x 6 plate. Then add the two 1 x 2 Technic bricks with X-shaped axle holes, a 2 x 4 brick and four 1 x 3 bricks.

STEP 8: Place the final 4 x 6 plate on top of Radio's head. Then gather the bricks shown for the rest of the head. Build the eyes by inserting a blue axle pin into each wheel.

STEP 9: Attach the eyes to the Technic bricks with an X-shaped axle hole. Build eyebrows by using 1 x 2 slope bricks with four slots. A steering wheel looks perfect on top of Radio's head!

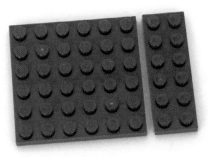

STEP 10: Build the body. Begin with a 6 x 6 plate and a 2 x 6 plate.

STEP 11: Add two 1 x 6 dark gray bricks and six 2 x 2 red inverted slopes.

STEP 12: Build two more layers of dark gray bricks. Place a 1 x 4 brick with four studs on the side on the front of the robot's body.

STEP 13: Attach a 1 x 6 red Technic brick on each side. Add two 1 x 2 red bricks and a 1 x 4 red brick. Gather the bricks shown for building the mechanism that will raise and lower Radio's head.

STEP 14: Slide the axle (10 studs long) through the center hole in each Technic brick, the 40-tooth gear and the two Technic bushes. Make sure that the axle goes through one of the four X-shaped axle holes on the edge of the gear—not the center hole! This is important for the motion of the head. Insert the blue pin with friction ridges into the 2 x 4 L-shaped liftarm, as shown.

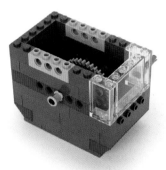

STEP 15: Attach the L-shaped liftarm to the black axle to create a handle.

STEP 16: Build two more layers on Radio's body. Add 1 x 4 Technic bricks to each side. Use clear panels in the front of the body if you want to be able to see the mechanism. Otherwise, just use regular bricks.

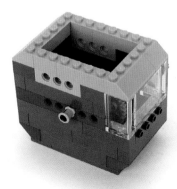

STEP 17: Add a 2 x 4 slope and a 2 x 2 slope to both the front and the back of the robot's body. Each side has a 1 x 2 brick and a 1 x 4 brick.

STEP 18: Add a layer of red bricks.

STEP 19: Now Radio needs a rod coming down from his head that will make it go up and down. Gather the bricks shown.

STEP 20: Attach the two 1 x 2 tan tiles and the two 1 x 2 x 1 red panels to the 2 x 4 light gray plate.

STEP 21: Turn the plate upside down and attach a 2 x 2 round brick. Then insert the axle (6 studs long).

STEP 22: Slide the red 4 x 4 round plate onto the axle—it should be able to spin freely. Then attach the remaining 2 x 2 round brick to the underside of Radio's head. Insert the other end of the axle into this brick.

STEP 23: Place Radio's head in the body cavity. It should rest on top of the 40-tooth gear. Then gather the bricks shown.

STEP 24: Use your finger to slide up the red 4 x 4 round plate. Attach a 2 x 6 dark gray plate to the front and the back of the neck opening. Between them add a 1 x 2 dark gray plate on each side. Then attach the red 4 x 4 round plate to these.

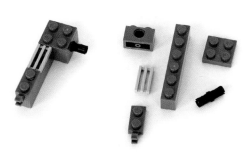

STEP 25: Build Radio's arms. Use a 2 x 2 plate to attach a 1 x 2 Technic brick to a 1 x 6 brick. Then add a 1 x 2 plate with a clip on the end and a 1 x 2 grill. Slide a black pin into the Technic brick.

STEP 26: Use the black pins to attach the arms to the body.

STEP 27: Build Radio's legs and feet. Each leg has a 2 x 4 dark gray brick and three 2 x 2 light gray bricks. Then add two 1 x 2 red slopes with four slots to each foot.

STEP 28: Attach the legs, and Radio is complete!

Make Radio's head move up and down by turning the handle on the side of his body!

MARVELOUS MINI ROBOTS

If you're in the mood to build something a little simpler than one of the mechanical robots, give these mini robots a try! How many different robot faces can you create with your bricks? Look for new ways to use your bricks. For example, little round plates can be used as eyes, but so can cones or even a phone handle.

HOW IT WORKS

Robots are often designed with two large wheels in the front, but a robot can't balance with only two wheels. Do you know why? If the robot's body tilted forward or backward at all, its center of gravity would change, the robot would be off-balance and it would fall over! Robots with two wheels in the front must be designed with one or two wheels in the back for stability.

Two-wheeled machines do exist, however! Segways and hoverboards keep their riders upright through the use of gyroscopic sensors inside them. Gyroscopes are spinning wheels that resist changes in their orientation. If the hoverboard tilts to one side, the gyroscope will stay upright, which prompts sensors to send a message to the wheels to move so that they stay under the rider's center of gravity. If the rider tilts forward, the wheels do too. The spinning motion of gyroscopes is also essential to keeping airplanes on course. Who knew a spinning wheel could be so useful?

PARTS LIST (FOR BUILDING THE BLUE AND WHITE ROLLING ROBOT)

WHITE BRICKS
3—2 x 4 plates
1—1 x 4 plate
4—1 x 2 plates
1—1 x 2 grill

BLUE BRICKS
2—2 x 2 plates
2—2 x 4 plates
2—2 x 4 bricks
2—1 x 2 plates
1—2 x 2 brick
1—2 x 4 vehicle mudguard

DARK GRAY BRICKS
2—1 x 2 plates with a ball on the end and a socket on the other end
2—1 x 2 plates with a ball on the side
1—1 x 2 plate
1—1 x 1 round tile
2—1 x 2 plates with a clip on the end

RED BRICKS
1—2 x 4 red plate
1—1 x 2 red plate
2—1 x 2 red slopes, 30 degree
2—1 x 2 red grill

ASSORTED BRICKS
2—1 x 2 light gray plates with a socket on the end
1—2 x 2 light gray brick with two pins
1—1 x 2—2 x 2 black bracket
2—1 x 1 black round plate
1—2 x 2 turntable
2—wheels
1—2 x 2 light gray airplane wheel
1—airplane tire
1—lever (antenna)

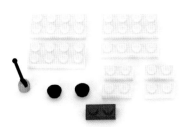

STEP 1: Find three 2 x 4 white plates, a 1 x 4 white plate, four 1 x 2 white plates, a 1 x 2 red plate, two 1 x 1 black round plates and a gray lever (antenna) for building the robot's head.

STEP 2: Attach a 1 x 2 red plate and three 1 x 2 white plates to a 2 x 4 white plate.

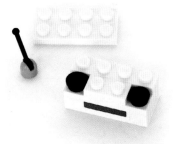

STEP 3: Add two 1 x 1 black round plates as eyes. Then add a 1 x 2 white plate and a 1 x 4 white plate.

STEP 4: Attach the last 2 x 4 white plate and give the robot an antenna.

STEP 5: Gather the bricks shown.

STEP 6: Attach the wheels to the 2 x 2 brick with two pins. Then attach the back wheels and the front airplane wheel to the 2 x 4 blue plate.

STEP 7: Add a 2 x 2 blue brick and a 2 x 2 blue plate.

STEP 8: Gather the bricks shown for building the robot's body.

STEP 9: Attach the 2 x 4 mudguard, and then place two 1 x 2 plates on top of that.

STEP 10: Stack a 2 x 4 blue brick, a 2 x 4 red plate and one more 2 x 4 blue brick. Add these to the body.

STEP 11: Attach a 1 x 2—2 x 2 black bracket to the front of the body. Then add two 1 x 2 dark gray plates with a ball on the side and a 1 x 2 dark gray plate.

STEP 12: Add a 2 x 4 blue plate, a 2 x 2 blue plate and a 2 x 2 turntable.

STEP 13: Attach the robot's head to the turntable.

STEP 14: Assemble the robot's arms as shown.

STEP 15: Connect the arms to the ball joints on the shoulders, and the robot is complete!

Now try building more robots on your own using these pictures of the finished projects. Or get creative and try building your own designs from scratch. On this cute little robot, use a phone handle to build the eyes.

The phone handle is held in place by a 1 x 1 plate with a clip on top. Use clips for the hands as well and he can hold a walkie talkie.

Use flick missiles to build the eyes on this robot and give him tiny wheels.

Attach the arms to a 4 x 4 black plate with octagonal bars. If you want, you can make him look super silly by adding extra arms!

See if you can use the pictures to build this classic-looking space robot.

He even has a jet pack on his back! These mini techno-bots are perfect for creating LEGO scenes. Try creating a computer workstation and a lab complete with tools and equipment for the robots to work in.

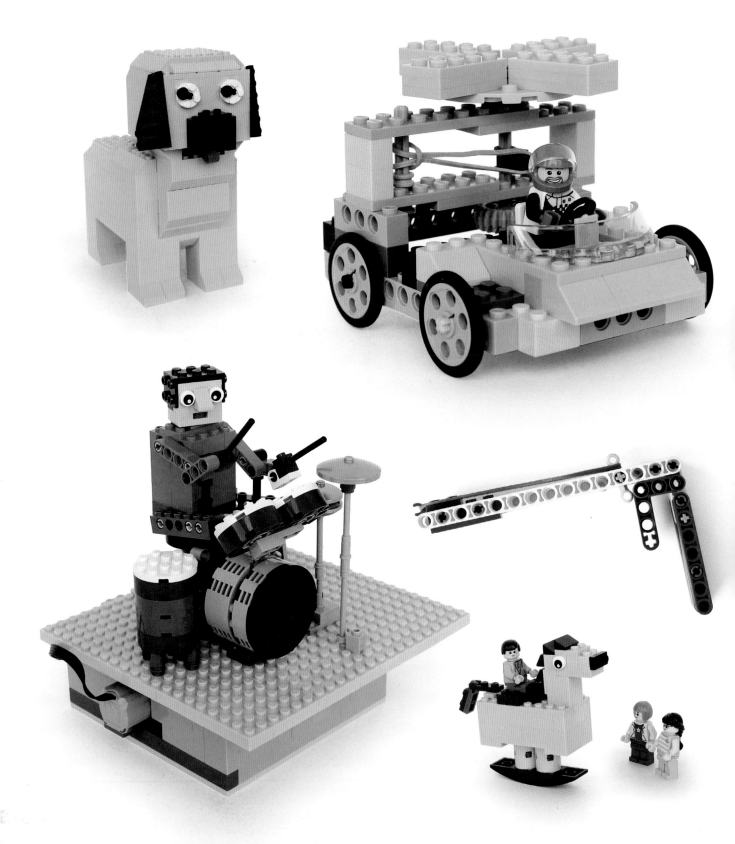

TERRIFIC MECHANICAL TOYS

Embrace the spirit of classic mechanical toys, but construct them out of LEGO bricks! Bricks prove to be surprisingly versatile in this exciting collection of projects. Build a drummer whose jointed arms actually play the drums. His limbs are animated with pistons that come up out of the floor! Use gears to create a dog that rolls his eyes while sticking out his tongue, build a working rubber band gun and so many more cool things. After creating all these mechanical toys, you just may be inspired to become a toy designer yourself!

FLYWHEEL CAR

Build a wind-up car with the added power of a flywheel. This fun toy uses a mechanism similar to the one inside a friction-drive car. You know those toy cars that you push along the floor a few times to rev up the wheels, and then you set them down and they roll on their own? The secret to those toys is a flywheel! This project will allow you to explore how that works. Wind up your fly car by turning the flywheel. The rubber band will wrap around the black Technic pole reverser handle. Keep winding until the rubber band is good and tight. Then let go and watch the car zoom away!

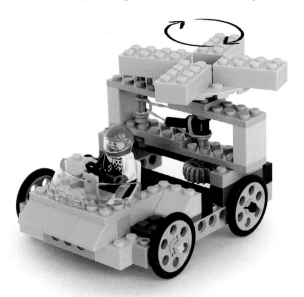 

HOW IT WORKS

A flywheel is a weighted wheel that uses inertia to keep something spinning. Inertia is an object's resistance to a change in motion. An object that is moving, and this includes spinning, will keep moving until another force stops it. Just like this LEGO car, friction-drive toys have a gear attached to the rear axle that turns a flywheel. When you push the car, the motion of the wheels starts the flywheel spinning. The flywheel keeps spinning even after you stop pushing the car, which keeps the wheels turning for longer than they would spin on their own.

Instead of using 2 x 4 bricks on your LEGO flywheel, use stacks of 2 x 4 plates for added weight. As you wind up the car, the rubber band stores up potential energy. Let the car go, and the car is propelled forward as the rubber band unwinds. Potential energy is converted to kinetic energy. In addition, inertia keeps the flywheel spinning even after the force from the rubber band has been spent, which keeps the car rolling for a longer distance. Test your car by winding it up and letting it go with the flywheel attached and then with the flywheel removed. It should roll farther with the flywheel!

DID YOU KNOW?

Flywheels are used in cars to make the engine run more smoothly as it's starting up and while the driver is not applying force to the gas pedal. The weight of the flywheel keeps it spinning at a constant speed, which smooths out the bursts of power created by the pistons. Without a flywheel, you would experience a really jerky ride!

PARTS LIST

LIGHT GRAY BRICKS
2—1 x 12 Technic bricks
1—1 x 6 Technic brick
2—1 x 4 Technic bricks
2—2 x 8 Technic plates
2—2 x 6 Technic plates
4—1 x 4 plates
1—Technic axle, 5 studs long
1—Technic axle, 7 studs long
2—Technic bevel gears, 20 tooth
2—Technic bushes, ½ length

YELLOW BRICKS
2—2 x 6 bricks
4—1 x 2 bricks
2—2 x 2 slopes

LIME GREEN BRICKS
1—2 x 6 plate
12—2 x 4 plates
2—1 x 4 bricks
3—2 x 2 slopes

ASSORTED BRICKS
2—1 x 10 black Technic bricks
1—black Technic axle, 12 studs long
1—4 x 10 dark gray plate

2—1 x 4 dark gray bricks
2—2 x 2 dark gray round plates
1—1 x 2 dark gray round tile with a hole
1—6 x 6 medium azure round plate
1—chair
1—steering wheel
1—Technic pole reverser handle (LEGO ID 6553)
2—tan Technic axle pins without friction ridges
4—wedge belt wheels with tires
1—3 x 6 x 1 curved windshield

OTHER ITEMS
1—rubber band

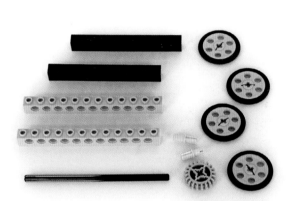

STEP 1: Gather the bricks shown for building the base of the car.

STEP 2: Use the two 1 x 10 black Technic bricks to connect the two 1 x 12 light gray Technic bricks. Slide a 20-tooth bevel gear onto the black axle (12 studs long) and then insert it into the light gray Technic bricks. Use the third hole from the end.

STEP 3: Slide the rear wheels onto the axle. Attach the front wheels to the car with two tan axle pins (axle on one side, pin on the other).

STEP 4: Attach a 4 x 10 dark gray plate to the front end of the car. This will strengthen the frame. Then gather the bricks shown.

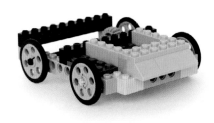

STEP 5: Attach two 2 x 6 yellow bricks to the underside of the dark gray plate. Then add two 1 x 4 lime green bricks and a 1 x 6 light gray Technic brick. Gather the bricks shown.

STEP 6: Attach three 2 x 2 lime green slopes to the underside of a 2 x 6 lime green plate. Attach this to the car on top of the 1 x 6 Technic brick. Then attach a 1 x 4 Technic brick underneath this, between the yellow bricks.

STEP 7: Stack two 1 x 4 light gray plates. Place the steering wheel on top of these and add it to the car. Then add a chair and a windshield.

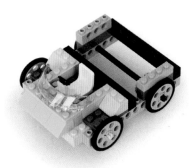

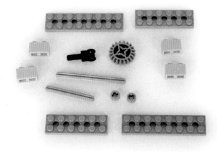

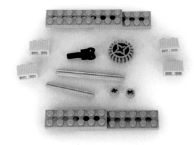

STEP 8: Add a 1 x 4 dark gray brick and a 1 x 4 light gray Technic brick on the right side of the car (top of the photo). Add a 1 x 4 dark gray brick and two 1 x 4 light gray plates on the left side of the car (bottom of the photo).

STEP 9: Gather the bricks shown for building the mechanism.

STEP 10: Connect the Technic plates as shown.

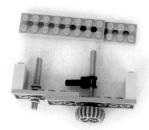

STEP 11: Slide an axle (7 studs long) through the fourth hole from the right. Add a 20-tooth bevel gear and a Technic pole reverser handle. Insert another axle (5 studs long) in the second hole from the left. Add a Technic bush (½ length) on both sides of the Technic plate. Add two 1 x 2 yellow bricks to both ends.

STEP 12: Attach the remaining two Technic plates on top. Then attach the mechanism to the car.

STEP 13: Add a 2 x 2 round tile with a hole in the center to the top of the axle (7 studs long). This will reduce friction between the flywheel and the car.

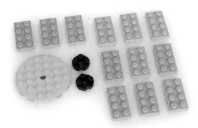 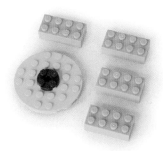 

STEP 14: Gather the bricks shown for building the flywheel. Use any color of plates if you don't have this many of one color.

STEP 15: Stack the 2 x 4 plates in groups of three. Attach a 2 x 2 dark gray round plate to both sides of a 6 x 6 round plate.

STEP 16: Attach the lime green plates to the 6 x 6 round plate. These add weight to the wheel.

STEP 17: Slide the flywheel onto the axle (7 studs long), and your car is just about ready!

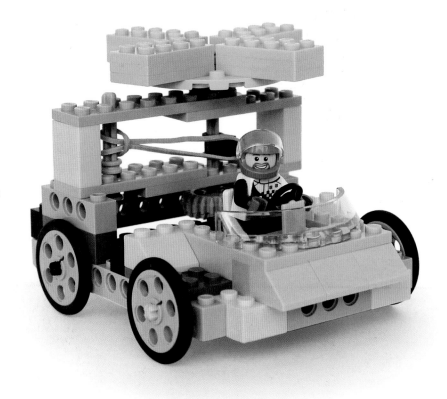

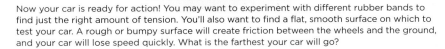

STEP 18: Attach the rubber band to the axle (5 studs long) using a loop knot. Then hook the other end around the black Technic pole reverser handle. You'll wind the car by turning the flywheel, and the rubber band will wrap around the black Technic pole reverser handle.

Now your car is ready for action! You may want to experiment with different rubber bands to find just the right amount of tension. You'll also want to find a flat, smooth surface on which to test your car. A rough or bumpy surface will create friction between the wheels and the ground, and your car will lose speed quickly. What is the farthest your car will go?

MONKEY LADDER

A monkey ladder is a classic toy that involves a wooden peg (sometimes decorated like a monkey) climbing down a ladder by flipping from one side, then to the other as it falls from rung to rung. It's quite fascinating to watch! Build your own brick version of this amusing toy and watch your "monkey" climb down the ladder again and again. Keep in mind that you may have to tighten up the connections in both the ladder and the monkey after a few runs by pushing down on the bricks. If the bricks start to separate, your monkey ladder won't perform as well.

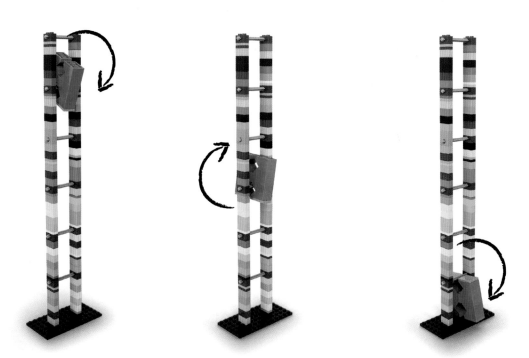

HOW IT WORKS

This project makes use of gravity and an object's center of gravity, or balance point, to create some really entertaining motion. The "monkey" spins around the rungs of the ladder, first one way and then the other until it gets to the bottom. Why does it do this? When you let go of the monkey, it hits the first rung at a point that is slightly off its center of gravity, so it pivots and turns upside down. When it hits the next rung, it strikes the rung at a point on the other side of its center of gravity and spins the other way.

Both the shape of the monkey and the dimensions of the ladder are critical to the toy's success. The shape of the monkey must allow it to pivot just the right amount as it falls from rung to rung. It must let go of one rung when it is perfectly lined up with the rung below it. The spacing between the rungs must be enough to give the monkey room to pivot, but not so much room that the monkey misses it altogether.

PARTS LIST

LADDER

6—Technic axles, 7 studs long
12—1 x 2 Technic bricks with an axle hole
60—1 x 2 bricks
24—1 x 2 plates
1—6 x 12 plate

MONKEY

2—2 x 3 plates
4—2 x 2 slopes
4—2 x 2 inverted slopes
8—1 x 2 bricks
1—2 x 4 brick
1—2 x 3 brick
1—2 x 6 plate
1—1 x 2 plate
4—1 x 3 light gray tiles

STEP 1: Build your ladder. Create two towers with five 1 x 2 bricks and two 1 x 2 plates in each. Place them four studs apart.

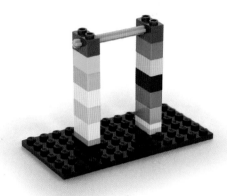

STEP 2: Add a 1 x 2 Technic brick with an X-shaped axle hole to each side. Slide an axle (7 studs long) through both bricks.

STEP 3: Continue building following the same pattern. Be sure that the distance between the rungs is five 1 x 2 bricks and two 1 x 2 plates. If you don't have enough bricks or axles, the toy will work with a shorter ladder.

STEP 4: Start building the "monkey" (it doesn't really look like a monkey) by gathering the bricks shown. Color is not important.

STEP 5: Place a 1 x 2 brick and a 2 x 2 slope on top of each 2 x 3 plate.

STEP 6: Add a 2 x 2 inverted slope and a 1 x 2 brick to each one. Then gather the bricks shown.

STEP 7: Attach the two sides with a 2 x 4 brick, a 2 x 3 brick, a 2 x 6 plate and a 1 x 2 plate.

STEP 8: Build two more layers on each side. The first is a 2 x 2 slope and a 1 x 2 brick. The second is a 2 x 2 inverted slope and a 1 x 2 brick. Then gather the bricks shown.

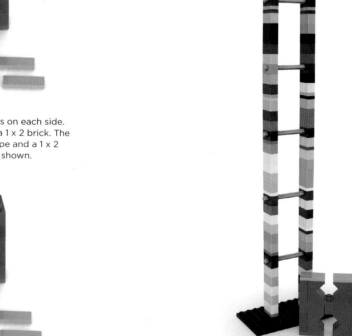

STEP 9: Finish up the monkey by placing two 1 x 3 tiles on each side.

Now you're ready to try out your monkey ladder! If you have trouble with the monkey falling off, check to be sure that all your bricks are connected tightly. Then make sure that the surface you are working on is flat. Most tables are not perfectly level! Try moving to a new location, or turn the monkey ladder a different direction on the table.

SILLY SPINNING FLOWER GARDEN

Build a silly garden with kittens and flowers that spin as they bob up and down. Simply turn the handle and watch your garden scene come to life! If flowers aren't your thing, try building a ninja battle. Once you have the hang of the basic cam and follower box, you can customize it and build all kinds of animated scenes.

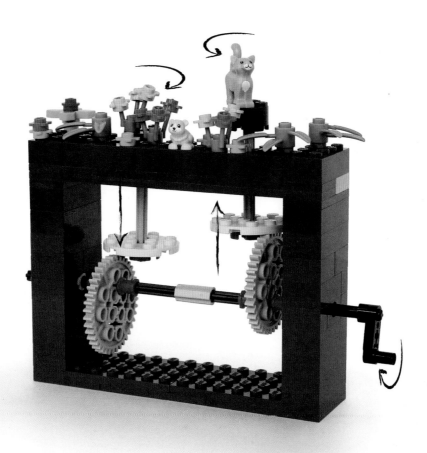

HOW IT WORKS

This project is a basic cam and follower construction. It's kind of cool how simple it is! When you turn the handle, the off-center gears bump into the followers (the yellow round plates) and make them move up and down. The followers are positioned so that the cams bump into them on one side rather than in the center, which makes them spin as they move up and down. It's a simple way to create motion, but cams and followers are used in so many devices, such as sewing machines and even the engine of a car.

PARTS LIST

BROWN BRICKS
2—4 x 8 plates
1—4 x 4 plate
2—4 x 6 plates
15—2 x 4 bricks
2—1 x 2 Technic bricks
5—1 x 2 bricks
2—1 x 4 bricks
1—2 x 3 brick
5—2 x 2 bricks
3—2 x 8 plates

4—2 x 4 plates
2—2 x 2 round bricks

LIGHT GRAY BRICKS
2—2 x 8 Technic plates
2—2 x 6 Technic plates
1—2 x 4 Technic plate
2—Technic bushes
2—Technic gears, 40 tooth
1—light gray Technic connector
2—light gray Technic axles, 7 studs long

ASSORTED BRICKS
2—black Technic axles, 10 studs long
4—red Technic bushes
1—1 x 3 black Technic liftarm with two axle holes and a pin/crank
2—2 x 2 dark gray round plates
2—4 x 4 yellow round plates
Flowers, plants and small animals, or various gray bricks, plants and ninja minifigures

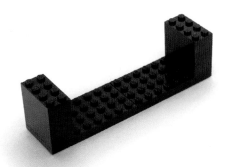

STEP 1: Build the base. Start by building two layers of brown plates. Attach two 4 x 8 plates to a 4 x 4 plate and two 4 x 6 plates. Then add three 2 x 4 bricks on each side.

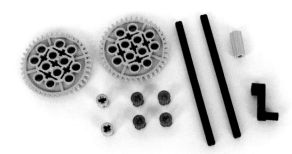

STEP 2: Gather the bricks shown for building the cams.

STEP 3: Connect the two axles (10 studs long) with a light gray connector. Then slide on the Technic bush and gears as shown. Place a 1 x 2 Technic brick on each side of the frame, then slide the axles through those. Secure them with two Technic bushes on one end and a handle on the other. The black handle is a 1 x 3 Technic liftarm with two axle holes and a pin/crank.

STEP 4: Add two 1 x 2 brown bricks on each side of the frame.

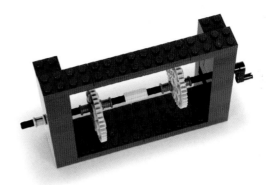

STEP 5: Build up the frame by adding three 2 x 4 bricks and two 2 x 2 bricks on each side. Then add a 2 x 4 plate on each side.

STEP 6: Build two layers of plates, 2 x 16 studs long to connect the top of the frame. The plates shown are two 2 x 8 plates on the bottom layer, then two 2 x 4 plates and a 2 x 8 plate on top.

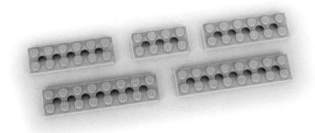

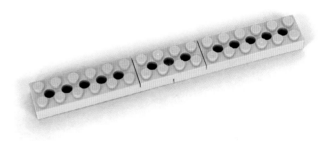

STEP 7: Gather the Technic plates shown. Substitute other colors if you need to.

STEP 8: Attach the Technic plates as shown.

STEP 9: Place your 2 x 16 section of Technic plates onto the frame. This will provide holes to run the pistons through.

STEP 10: Gather the bricks for the pistons. You'll need two light gray axles (7 studs long), two 2 x 2 dark gray round plates and two 4 x 4 yellow round plates. Or substitute other colors.

STEP 11: Turn the yellow plates upside down and attach a 2 x 2 round plate to each one. Then insert the light gray axles.

STEP 12: Slide the axles through the holes in the Technic bricks. The easiest way to do this is to detach the yellow plates, slide the axles through the holes, then attach the yellow round plates again. Note that the yellow round plates have round holes, so the axles won't attach to them. The 2 x 2 dark gray round plates have an X-shaped axle hole and will hold onto the axles.

STEP 13: Place a 2 x 2 round brick on top of each light gray axle. Try turning the handle. The brown round bricks shown bob up and down and turn. Notice that they turn in opposite directions because the cams are bumping them on opposite sides.

Now that your frame is complete, it's time to add a fun scene! Add plants, flowers and small animals. Kittens, bunnies and hamsters are cute in the middle of the garden!

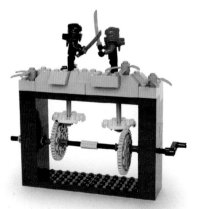

Turn the handle, and the kitten and the orange flowers will move up and down and spin.

Or try building a ninja duel! Add some gray bricks and slopes to the top of the frame, with a few plants also. Then add some ninja minifigures with swords. Which ninja will come out on top?

POWER SHOT RUBBER BAND GUN

You have probably seen those classic wooden guns that shoot a rubber band when you pull the trigger. Well, now you can build one with LEGO bricks! Because of the strength needed to withstand the tension of the rubber band, you'll need to use Technic liftarms connected with pins. The completed toy is easy to load and shoot, and it has a satisfying amount of power! Load the gun by hooking a rubber band around the clip at the front and the knob wheel in the back. Make sure that the trigger is in its "up" position. Pull down on the trigger, and the rubber band will go flying!

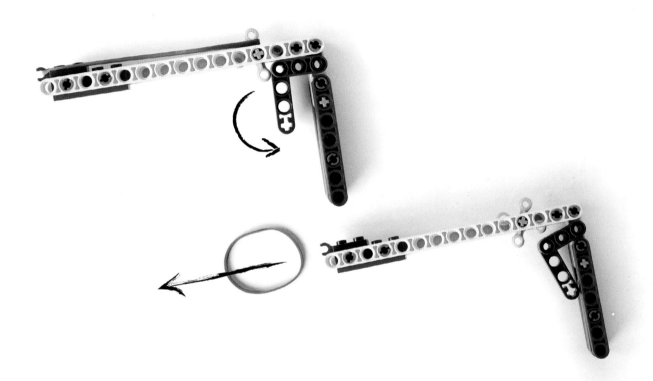

HOW IT WORKS

The trigger in this gun pivots up and down. When you push the trigger up, it will hold the knob wheel in place. Pull the trigger down, and the knob wheel will spin from the tension of the rubber band, which sends the rubber band flying! When you stretch the rubber band from the clip at the front to the knob wheel at the back, it gains potential energy, or stored energy. As soon as you release the trigger, that stored energy is converted to kinetic energy, or the energy of motion! Try experimenting with different sizes and thicknesses of rubber bands until you find one that shoots the farthest.

PARTS LIST

ASSORTED BRICKS
2—1 x 15 white Technic liftarms
2—1 x 7 red Technic liftarms
1—1 x 5 blue Technic liftarm
1—2 x 4 white L-shaped Technic liftarm, thick
1—2 x 4 dark gray L-shaped Technic liftarm, thick
1—1 x 3 dark gray Technic liftarm
1—1 x 4 red Technic brick
2—light gray Technic axles, 3 studs long
1—yellow Technic knob wheel
3—black Technic pins
6—blue Technic pins, 3 studs long with friction ridges
1—1 x 2 dark gray plate with a clip on the end

OTHER ITEMS
1—rubber band

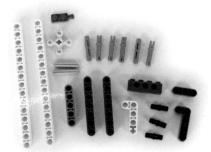

STEP 1: Gather the bricks shown for building the rubber band gun.

STEP 2: Attach an L-shaped liftarm to a 1 x 15 liftarm by connecting it with two pins (3 studs long). The pins will go through both liftarms and then stick out at the top.

STEP 3: Use two blue pins (3 studs long) to attach a 1 x 4 red Technic brick at the front of the gun. Slide an axle (3 studs long) through the fourth hole from the back. Then slide the knob wheel onto the axle.

STEP 4: Connect a second 1 x 15 white liftarm to the gun. Then insert 3 black pins into a 1 x 3 dark gray liftarm.

STEP 5: Attach the 1 x 3 dark gray liftarm to the dark gray L-shaped liftarm to create the trigger. Then connect this to the gun. Insert a light gray axle (3 studs long) into the white liftarm. Then build the handle of the gun as shown. Attach the handle by sliding the top blue pin into the hole above the light gray axle. Then attach the second red liftarm.

Pivot the trigger up to lock the knob wheel in place, and then load a rubber band. Now it's time to have some fun! Try building some LEGO targets to shoot with your rubber band gun.

ANIMATED DRUMMER

Build a LEGO guy that really plays the drums! Watch his arms hit the drums and cymbals as his right foot keeps time with a base drum pedal on the floor. This project is motorized, so all you have to do is turn him on and watch him go. Turn on some music for him to play along with! After that, you might be inspired to build other instruments for a band. How about designing a guitar player to match?

This drummer is a more advanced project than many of the others in this book, but if you love mechanical parts (and drums!) it will be well worth your effort to build it. It's truly a project to display and enjoy for a long time to come, which just goes to show that good engineering is more than mechanical parts and pieces. The right design can bring a smile to the face of anyone who sees it!

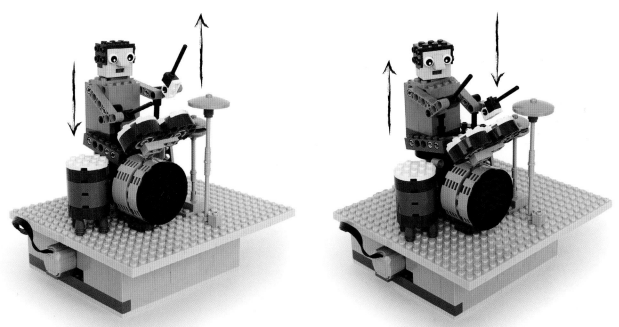

HOW IT WORKS

The trick to making this LEGO drummer move is two cams and sliders that are hidden under the platform that he sits on. The cams act as cranks, and they drive the sliders (Technic axles) in an assembly called a slider-crank linkage. When you switch on the motor, the motor spins an 8-tooth gear on an axle. The 8-tooth gear then turns a 24-tooth gear. It's necessary to "gear down" a little, or the speed of the motor would cause the drummer to play so fast that pieces would go flying off! The 24-tooth gear turns an axle with a 1 x 2 liftarm connected to a 1 x 3 liftarm. As the liftarms spin, they act as cranks, creating the up-and-down motion of the sliders.

The sliders come up out of the floor and attach to the arms and right leg of the drummer. In fact, the first slider operates both the right arm and right leg while the second operates his left arm.

PARTS LIST

DRUMMER GUY

TAN BRICKS
1—2 x 3 plate
2—1 x 2 plates
1—1 x 1 plate
2—1 x 3 plates
1—1 x 2 slope
2—1 x 1 bricks with a stud on the side

BLUE BRICKS
7—2 x 4 bricks
2—1 x 4 Technic bricks
1—2 x 4 plate
2—1 x 5 Technic liftarms
2—1 x 3 Technic liftarms

DARK GRAY BRICKS
1—1 x 4 plate
1—2 x 3 plate
1—1 x 2—1 x 2 hinge plate
1—1 x 2 plate
1—1 x 1 plate
2—1 x 2 bricks
1—1 x 4 brick
1—1 x 4 Technic brick
2—1 x 6 Technic bricks
1—1 x 7 Technic liftarm

BROWN BRICKS
2—1 x 3 plates
1—1 x 2 plate
2—1 x 2—2 x 2 brackets
1—1 x 3 brick
2—1 x 1 bricks with a stud on the side

ASSORTED BRICKS
2—eyes
1—1 x 1 red round plate
1—2 x 2 dark tan tile with one stud on top
4—black Technic pins with friction ridges
4—light gray Technic pins
1—1 x 2 white plate with a pin hole on top
2—black bars, 4 studs long
1—2 x 2 light gray round brick

STOOL
1—4 x 4 black round brick
2—2 x 2 dark gray round bricks
1—2 x 2 dark gray brick
1—light gray Technic axle, 5 studs long

DRUMS

LIGHT GRAY BRICKS
8—6 x 6 round plates
1—2 x 2 plate
1—2 x 3 plate
1—1 x 4 plate
3—bars, 6 studs long with a stop ring
2—2 x 2 round bricks
1—2 x 2 brick modified with top pin and 1 x 2 side plates
1—1 x 1 brick with a clip on the side
1—1 x 2 plate with two fingers
1—Technic pin, ½ length with 2-stud long bar extension (flick missile)
1—Technic pin

DARK GRAY BRICKS
3—4 x 4 round bricks
3—2 x 2 round bricks
4—1 x 1 cones
4—1 x 1 round plates
1—2 x 2 plate
1—1 x 1 round brick
2—1 x 2 plates with two fingers
3—1 x 2 plates with one finger

ASSORTED BRICKS
1—2 x 4 black plate
2—6 x 6 black round plates
4—4 x 4 white round plates
16—2 x 2 dark red round corner bricks
2—3 x 3 metallic gold dishes
1—2 x 4 tan plate
1—4 x 4 gold dish

BASE
1—16 x 16 tan plate
Various gray bricks
Various tan bricks
Tan plates, or supplement with other colors
2—2 x 3 bricks, any color

MECHANISM

LIGHT GRAY BRICKS
3—1 x 2 Technic bricks with two holes
1—1 x 2 brick, two bricks high
2—Technic axles, 3 studs long
1—Technic axle, 7 studs long
1—Technic bush
1—1 x 5 Technic liftarm
2—1 x 3 Technic liftarms
2—1 x 2 Technic liftarms with a pin hole and an axle hole
1—1 x 2 plate with a clip on top
1—1 x 2 plate with a handle on the end
9—Technic pins
1—Technic connector #6
2—Technic connector #1

DARK GRAY BRICKS
3—1 x 2 Technic bricks with two holes
1—1 x 7 Technic liftarm
1—Technic connectors #1
3—Technic gears, 8 tooth
2—Technic gears, 24 tooth

ASSORTED BRICKS
1—red Technic axle, 2 studs long with notches
1—tan Technic axle pin
2—black Technic connectors #1
1—black Technic pin connector, 2 studs long with slot
1—black Technic axle connector with axle hole
2—black Technic axles, 3 studs long
1—black Technic axle, 12 studs long
1—black Technic pin
1—dark tan axle, 3 studs long with a stud on the end
1—red Technic bush

OTHER ITEMS
AAA battery box
M-motor

BUILDING TIPS

If you let your drummer run for more than a few minutes at a time, some of the bricks may come loose and need to be tightened up again before his next performance. Also, the machine runs best when the pistons are attached to the drummer. When they are attached, their motion is restricted somewhat. If you run the motor without hooking up everything first, the pistons will wiggle around and pull the mechanism apart.

STEP 1: Start with the drummer guy. Place two 1 x 2 tan plates, a 1 x 1 tan plate and a 1 x 1 red round plate on top of a 2 x 3 tan plate.

STEP 2: Add a 1 x 3 tan plate and a 1 x 3 brown brick.

STEP 3: Add a 1 x 3 brown plate to his hair. Then add a 1 x 2 tan slope and two 1 x 1 tan bricks with a stud on the side. Attach the eyes.

STEP 4: Place a 1 x 3 tan plate over the eyes and another 1 x 3 brown plate on the hair. Find a 1 x 2 brown plate and two 1 x 2—2 x 2 brown brackets.

STEP 5: Attach the brackets and 1 x 2 plate to complete the drummer's hair.

STEP 6: Start building the drummer's body by stacking six 2 x 4 blue bricks.

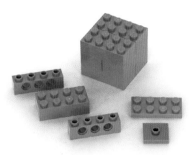

STEP 7: Gather the bricks shown.

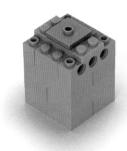

STEP 8: Attach the bricks as shown. The 2 x 2 dark tan tile with one stud on top will hold the drummer's head.

STEP 9: Insert a light gray pin on each side of the body. Then build the arms by connecting a 1 x 5 blue liftarm to a 1 x 3 blue liftarm with a black pin.

STEP 10: Attach the arms to the body. Connect the drumsticks to the arms by inserting a bar (4 studs long) into a 1 x 1 brown brick with a stud on the side. The left drumstick is attached to a 1 x 2 white plate with a pin hole, while the right drumstick is not. The purpose of this difference is to make the arms the right length to hit the drums and cymbal.

STEP 11: Turn the drummer over. Add a 1 x 4 plate, a 2 x 3 plate, a 1 x 2 plate, a 1 x 1 plate and a 1 x 2—1 x 2 hinge plate to the underside of his torso.

STEP 12: Add a 1 x 4 Technic brick, two 1 x 2 bricks and a 1 x 4 brick. Then place a 2 x 2 round brick in the center. The 2 x 2 round brick is vital for attaching the drummer to his seat.

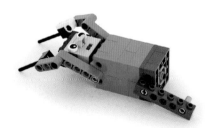

STEP 13: Build the right leg using a 1 x 6 Technic brick and two light gray pins.

STEP 14: The left leg is a little different. Attach a 1 x 6 Technic brick to a 1 x 7 liftarm using a black pin.

STEP 15: Attach the leg to the hinge plate.

STEP 16: Gather the bricks shown for building the drummer's stool.

STEP 17: Stack the bricks as shown and slide the light gray axle (5 studs long) down through the top three bricks.

STEP 18: Attach the drummer to the stool by sliding the light gray axle in the stool into the 2 x 2 round brick in his body.

STEP 19: Build some drums. Build a snare drum with a 4 x 4 white round plate, a 4 x 4 dark gray round brick and three 2 x 2 dark gray round bricks. Build a floor tom with a 4 x 4 white round plate, eight 2 x 2 dark red round corner bricks and two 4 x 4 dark gray round bricks. Use four 1 x 1 cones and four 1 x 1 round plates for the feet on the drum.

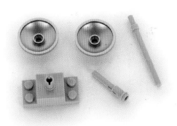

STEP 20: Gather the bricks shown for building the hi-hat.

STEP 21: Insert the gray pin (flick missile) into the 2 x 2 brick with a pin on top. Slide the metallic gold dishes onto the light gray bar (6 studs long), and then slide the bar into the top of the gray pin (flick missile).

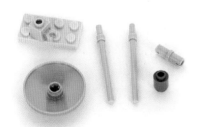

STEP 22: Gather the bricks shown for building the crash cymbal.

STEP 23: Build the crash cymbal as shown. Use the gray pin to connect two light gray bars (6 studs long). Note that the 2 x 4 tan plate is just holding up the cymbal and won't be used in the project.

STEP 24: Build the base drum. Start with a 6 x 6 black round plate and add a stack of five 6 x 6 light gray round plates. If you don't have enough of the round plates, make the drum a little thinner.

STEP 25: Add two 1 x 2 dark gray plates with two fingers, a 1 x 2 dark gray plate with one finger, a 2 x 2 light gray plate and a 2 x 3 light gray plate.

STEP 26: Attach two 1 x 2 dark gray plates with one finger, and then add a 1 x 2 light gray plate with two fingers. Then find a 1 x 4 light gray plate and a 2 x 2 dark gray plate.

STEP 27: Complete the drum with three more 6 x 6 light gray round plates and a final 6 x 6 black round plate. Place the 2 x 2 dark gray plate on the bottom of the 1 x 2 dark gray plates with one finger. The 1 x 4 light gray plate goes on top of the bass drum to hold the toms.

STEP 28: Build the toms as shown.

STEP 29: Attach the toms to the 1 x 4 light gray plate.

STEP 30: Turn the drums around and add a 2 x 4 black plate to the drum head.

STEP 31: Start building the base for the drummer. Grab a 16 x 16 plate and add bricks as shown. It doesn't matter if all the colors match or not.

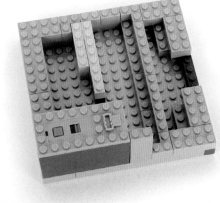

STEP 32: Attach the battery box in the corner and place two 1 x 2 bricks (two bricks high) next to it.

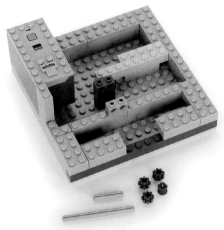

STEP 33: Add a 1 x 2 dark gray Technic brick with two holes, a 1 x 2 dark gray brick (two bricks high) and a 1 x 2 light gray Technic brick with two holes. Then find the bricks shown.

STEP 34: Insert the light gray axles and add the gears and Technic bush as shown.

STEP 35: Place a 1 x 2 dark gray Technic brick with two holes next to the 1 x 2 light gray Technic brick with two holes. Insert one black pin. Then gather the bricks shown.

STEP 36: Slide the dark tan axle (3 studs long) through the other hole in the 1 x 2 dark gray Technic brick. Add a 24-tooth Technic gear.

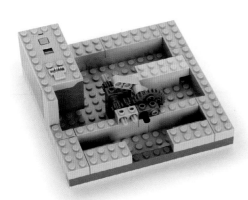

STEP 37: Use the dark tan axle to attach the 1 x 2 liftarm. Then use the light gray pin to connect the 1 x 3 liftarm to the 1 x 2 liftarm.

STEP 38: Connect the motor to the two light gray axles and the black pin. Then find the bricks shown.

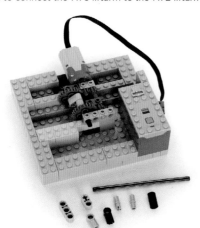

STEP 39: Add a 1 x 2 light gray brick (two bricks high) and two 1 x 2 Technic bricks with two holes. Then insert the black axle (3 studs long) and connect the 24-tooth Technic gear. The motor should now spin both axles that are attached to it. Then grab the bricks shown.

STEP 40: Slide the 1 x 2 liftarm onto the black axle (12 studs long). Then use a gray pin to connect the 1 x 3 liftarm to the 1 x 2 liftarm.

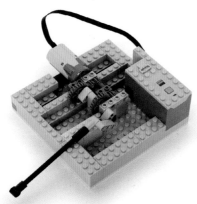

STEP 41: Use the final gray pin to attach a light gray Technic connector #1. Slide a black pin connector onto the black axle (12 studs long), and then insert it into the light gray connector #1. Add the black connector #1 on top. The pin connector will give the piston a little extra stability so that it won't rattle around while it goes up and down.

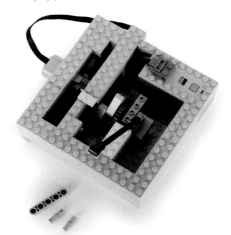

STEP 42: Add bricks so that each wall is the same height as the battery box. Add a 1 x 2 tan plate. Then find a 1 x 5 liftarm and two gray pins.

STEP 43: Use a gray pin to attach the 1 x 5 liftarm to the first piston. Insert the other gray pin in the top hole of the 1 x 5 liftarm.

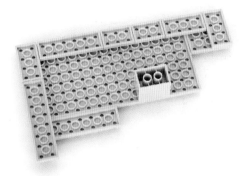

STEP 44: Build the top of the platform by creating a section of attached plates as shown. The two 2 x 3 bricks are very important to the mechanism. They will sit between the second piston and the wall of the base to keep it running smoothly.

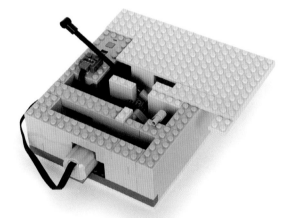

STEP 45: Attach the platform to the frame. Note the position of the two 2 x 3 bricks. Add two 1 x 3 bricks in front of the battery box to connect the two 1 x 2 Technic bricks with two holes.

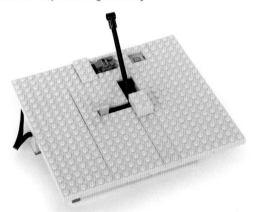

STEP 46: Add plates to the rest of the platform. Place a 2 x 3 brick in front of the black axle (12 studs long).

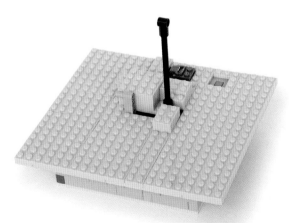

STEP 47: Add bricks for the drummer's stool to sit on. Behind the gray piston, add a 2 x 6 brick, a 2 x 4 brick and two 4 x 4 plates. Behind the black piston, add a 2 x 3 brick and a 2 x 3 plate.

STEP 48: Place the drummer and his stool on the platform. Use a light gray pin to attach his arm to the black piston. Add a 1 x 2 brick in front of the gray piston.

STEP 49: Gather the bricks shown for building the bass drum pedal and the drummer's right leg. Insert a light gray axle (3 studs long) and a red axle (2 studs long with notches) into a light gray connector #6.

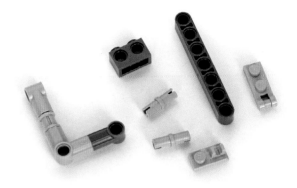

STEP 50: Slide on a Technic bush, a light gray connector #1 and a dark gray connector #1.

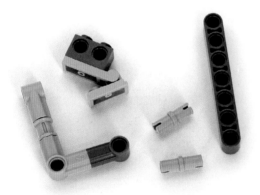

STEP 51: Attach a 1 x 2 Technic brick with two holes to a 1 x 2 plate with a handle on the end. Attach the handle to a 1 x 2 plate with a clip on top.

STEP 52: Use a light gray pin to attach the drum pedal to the 1 x 2 Technic brick with two holes.

STEP 53: Grab the final gray pin and attach the bottom of the drummer's leg to the bass drum pedal. Then attach the lower leg to the drummer's knee. Attach the 1 x 2 plate with a clip on top to the base.

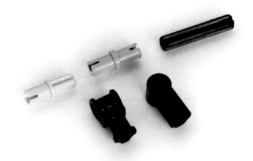

STEP 54: Grab the bricks shown to build a connection between the drummer's right arm and right leg. This will cause them to move together.

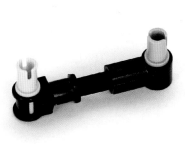

STEP 55: Connect them as shown.

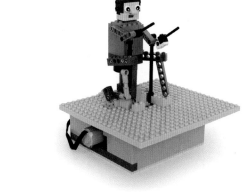

STEP 56: Insert the tan pin into the drummer's leg and the gray pin into his arm. Now his arm and leg will move up and down in unison as the light gray piston moves up and down from the floor.

STEP 57: Place the snare drum on top of a 2 x 3 brick and a 2 x 2 brick.

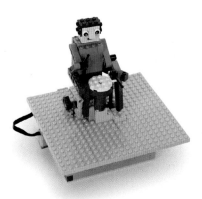

STEP 58: Attach the snare drum to the base between the drummer's legs.

STEP 59: Then arrange the bass drum, toms and cymbals around the drummer.

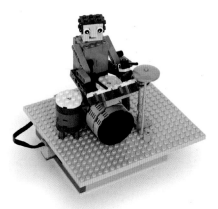

Your drummer is now complete, and you are ready to show him off! Turn on some music and let him play along to the beat!

ROSIE THE ROCKING HORSE

Give Rosie a push, and she will rock back and forth for a long time. You may think that it's a piece of cake to design a rocking horse, but not so fast! It's important to have the center of gravity in the right spot. Otherwise the poor rider might end up landing on her nose when the rocking horse tips over because of the weight of the horse's head. Pay careful attention to design, and your rocking horse will rock great!

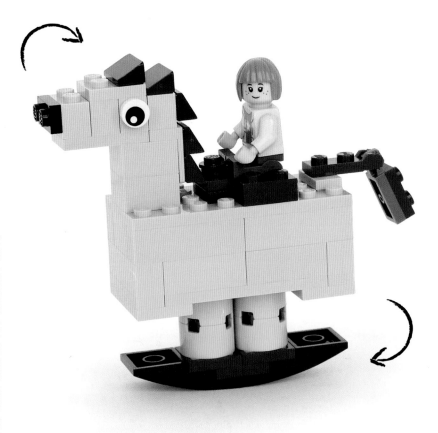

HOW IT WORKS

Toys like rocking horses need to be properly balanced to be safe to ride. To compensate for the extra weight at the front of the rocking horse (because of the head), you'll need to add weight to the back of the horse. This can easily be accomplished by making the body of the horse hollow. You can stack plates inside the body to add extra weight just where you want it.

When you add weight to the back, you are changing the rocking horse's center of gravity, or balance point. A real rocking horse will not tip forward like this LEGO one because of the weight of the child riding on it, but it still needs to be designed correctly. A real rocking horse will tip easily if the runners are not long enough. Can you think of other things that need to be properly balanced so that they don't tip over?

PARTS LIST

TAN BRICKS
1—4 x 8 plate
1—4 x 6 plate
2—2 x 4 plates
2—1 x 4 plates
1—2 x 3 plate
1—2 x 2 plate
2—1 x 6 bricks
6—1 x 4 bricks
2—2 x 2 bricks
3—1 x 2 bricks
2—1 x 2 bricks with two studs on the side

4—2 x 2 round bricks
2—1 x 1 bricks with one stud on the side
1—1 x 2 plate with one stud on top
1—1 x 2—2 x 2 bracket

BROWN BRICKS
1—2 x 4 plate
2—2 x 2 plates
6—1 x 2 plates
5—1 x 2 slopes, 30 degree
1—1 x 2 hinge plate with two fingers
1—1 x 2 plate with one stud on top
1—1 x 1 round plate

ASSORTED BRICKS
2—2 x 4 dark brown curved slopes
1—1 x 2 dark gray hinge plate with one finger
1—1 x 2 black plate
2—eyes
6—2 x 2 plates, any color
6—1 x 2 plates, any color
2—red Technic axles, 2 studs long with notches

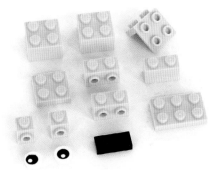

STEP 1: Gather the bricks shown for building Rosie's head.

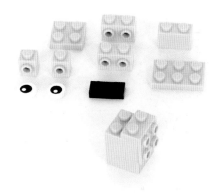

STEP 2: Stack two 2 x 2 bricks and place a 1 x 2—2 x 2 bracket on top.

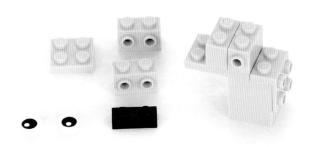

STEP 3: Add a 2 x 3 plate. Then add two 1 x 1 bricks with a stud on the side and a 1 x 2 brick in front of those.

STEP 4: Add two 1 x 2 bricks with two studs on the side. Place a 2 x 2 plate on top of the head. Add the eyes. Then add a 1 x 2 black plate for the nose.

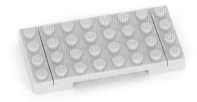

STEP 5: Use five 1 x 2 brown slopes to create the horse's mane.

STEP 6: Find the plates shown.

STEP 7: Attach the plates as shown to build the bottom of the horse's body.

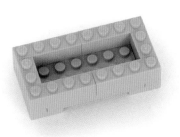

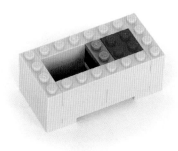

STEP 8: Add four 1 x 4 bricks and two 1 x 2 bricks.

STEP 9: Place two more 1 x 4 bricks and two 1 x 6 bricks on the body. Then build weights to put inside the body. Stack six 2 x 2 plates and six 1 x 2 plates.

STEP 10: Attach the weights to the back of the body.

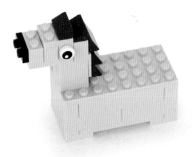

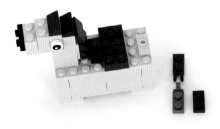

STEP 11: Cover the body with a 4 x 8 plate. Then attach Rosie's head to her body.

STEP 12: Build a saddle with a 2 x 4 plate and two 1 x 2 plates. Then gather the bricks shown.

STEP 13: Add a 1 x 2 plate, a 1 x 2 plate with one stud on top and a 1 x 1 round plate to the saddle. Then attach a 1 x 2 tan plate with one stud on top to hold the tail. Then gather the bricks shown.

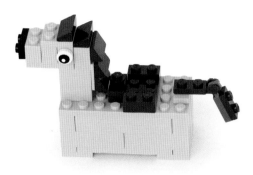

STEP 14: Build the tail as shown.

STEP 15: Gather the bricks shown for building Rosie's legs and runners. You will need two sets of these bricks.

STEP 16: Attach the brown plates to the underside of the dark brown curved slope. Insert a red Technic axle (2 studs long) in the underside of a 2 x 2 tan round brick. This will allow you to attach two 2 x 2 round bricks with the bottom sides together.

STEP 17: Build the second leg and runner.

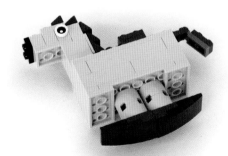

STEP 18: Attach the legs to the underside of Rosie's body, and your rocking horse is complete!

Find some minifigures who want to go for a ride! They'll probably have to take turns.

ROVER THE EYE-ROLLING DOG

This dog has a silly expression on his face, but he does more than just look silly! Turn the knob on the back of his head, and his eyes roll while his tongue moves in and out of his mouth. It's a clever mechanism, and it's totally cool that you can get LEGO bricks to do that! If you don't have enough bricks to build the body of the dog, try building just the head. Substitute colors if you don't have that much tan.

HOW IT WORKS

Rover's eyes both have gears behind them, and they are driven by a third gear in between the eyes. When you turn the knob on the back of Rover's head, the center gear turns in the same direction, which causes both eyes to turn at the same time in the opposite direction.

The brown knob also turns a worm gear. A worm gear is a shaft with threads like a screw. When they are connected with another gear, they change the direction of motion in a machine. The worm gear connects with an 8-tooth gear and converts the circular motion of the knob to the side-to-side motion (known as "lateral" motion) needed to make the tongue go in and out of the mouth. You'll need to turn the knob one way to make the tongue come out, and then the other way to make it go back in again.

PARTS LIST

TAN BRICKS
1—2 x 8 brick
7—2 x 6 bricks
6—2 x 4 bricks
4—1 x 4 bricks
2—1 x 6 bricks
4—1 x 3 bricks
8—1 x 2 bricks
6—2 x 2 slopes
2—1 x 2 slopes
8—2 x 2 inverted slopes
1—4 x 6 plate
2—2 x 6 plates
2—1 x 6 plates
1—2 x 2 plate
2—1 x 2 plates
3—1 x 2 Technic bricks
2—1 x 1 bricks with a stud on the side
4—1 x 1 bricks
3—1 x 2 slopes, 30 degree
Various tan bricks and plates for building the dog's body

BLACK BRICKS
2—6 x 6 wedge plates, cut corner
2—Technic axles, 4 studs long
1—Technic axle, 6 studs long
1—1 x 2 plate
2—1 x 1 round plates
1—1 x 2—2 x 2 bracket

LIGHT GRAY BRICKS
1—Technic axle, 5 studs long
3—Technic gears, 16 tooth
3—Technic bushes
4—Technic bushes, ½ length
1—Technic worm gear
1—1 x 2 Technic brick with two holes
1—1 x 3 Technic liftarm with two axle holes and a pin/crank

BROWN BRICKS
1—2 x 2 round brick
1—2 x 4 brick
2—2 x 2 inverted slopes
1—2 x 4 plate

ASSORTED BRICKS
1—1 x 7 red Technic liftarm
2—2 x 2 white round plates
1—Technic gear, 8 tooth

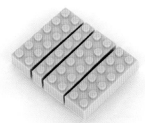

STEP 1: Line up a 2 x 6 brick, a 1 x 6 brick and two more 2 x 6 bricks.

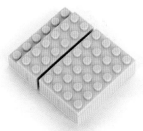

STEP 2: Add a 4 x 6 plate and a 2 x 6 plate.

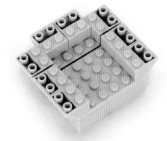

STEP 3: Use eight 2 x 2 inverted slopes to build a row around the sides and back of the dog's head.

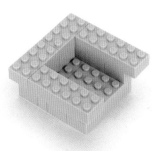

STEP 4: Add two 2 x 6 bricks and two 2 x 4 bricks.

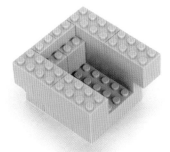

STEP 5: Build the next row with four 2 x 4 bricks and two 1 x 2 bricks.

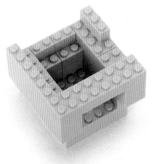

STEP 6: Place a 2 x 8 brick across the front of the dog's head. Then add a 1 x 2 brick and a 1 x 4 brick on the left side. Place a 1 x 3 brick at the back of the right side.

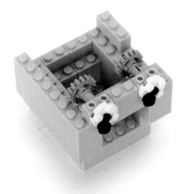

STEP 7: Gather the bricks shown for building the eyes. You will need two sets of these.

STEP 8: Slide the black axle (4 studs long) through the Technic brick and attach the 1 x 1 black round plate to the white 2 x 2 round plate to build the eye. Then slide the Technic bush and 16-tooth gear onto the axle behind the Technic brick.

STEP 9: Build the second eye. Attach the eyes to the head with a 1 x 2 brick between them.

STEP 10: Gather the bricks shown for building the tongue mechanism.

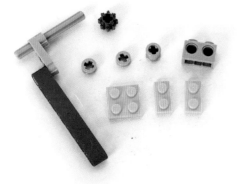

STEP 11: Insert the pin on the 1 x 3 liftarm into the red liftarm. Then add a light gray axle (5 studs long).

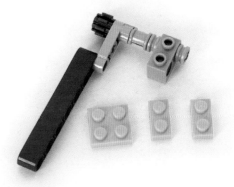

STEP 12: Slide on the 8-tooth gear, Technic bush, Technic bush (½ length), Technic brick with two holes and a final Technic bush (½ length).

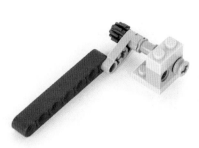

STEP 13: Stack two 1 x 2 tan plates and place them on top of the Technic brick. Attach a 2 x 2 tan plate underneath.

STEP 14: Attach the tongue assembly to the left side of the dog's head (right side of the picture). Nothing moves yet, but we are making progress!

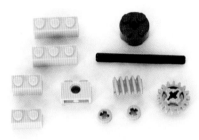

STEP 15: Gather the bricks shown.

STEP 16: Load up the black axle (6 studs long) with a 16-tooth gear, then a Technic bush (½ length), a Technic worm gear and finally another Technic bush (½ length). Stack the tan bricks as shown.

STEP 17: Slide the axle through the hole in the Technic brick, and then attach the assembly to the head. Add a 2 x 2 brown round brick. Try turning the round brick! The eyes should roll as the tongue moves. It's fun to watch how it works before you cover it up with bricks.

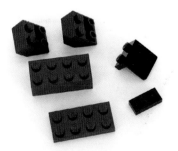

STEP 18: Gather the bricks shown for building the dog's nose.

STEP 19: Stack the brown bricks as shown.

STEP 20: Use the black bracket and 1 x 2 black plate to build the nose.

STEP 21: Attach the nose to the face. Rover looks much more like a dog now.

STEP 22: Add more tan bricks to the head. You'll need to leave a gap on each side so that the gears have room to turn, but the ears will cover up the gaps.

STEP 23: Build a final layer of tan bricks on the sides and back of the dog. There is a 1 x 2 slope on the back on each side. Note the position of the 1 x 1 bricks with one stud on the side—one on each side of the head. Add two 1 x 6 plates above the eyes.

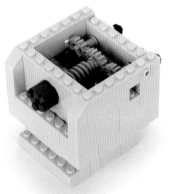

STEP 24: Check to be sure that your dog matches the picture.

STEP 25: Place a 2 x 6 plate above the eyes.

STEP 26: Complete the head with three 2 x 2 slopes on each side and two 2 x 6 bricks in the middle. Add three 1 x 2 slopes (30 degree) to the front of the head. Then find two 6 x 6 wedge plates with cut corners.

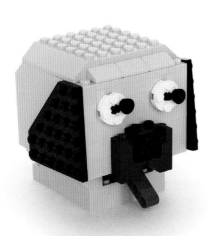

STEP 27: Attach the ears to the sides of the head, and Rover's head is complete!

Use the picture to design a body for Rover. The body is hollow, which reduces the number of bricks you'll need. If you don't have that many tan bricks, try making him a spotted dog with white, brown and black!

CURIOUS CONTRAPTIONS

Everyone knows that LEGO bricks can be used to build cars, spaceships, houses, forts and things like that. But how about machines that really do something—do you think your LEGO bricks can do that? Oh yes, they can! Here's a collection of amazing contraptions that you can build yourself without having to own millions of bricks. Along the way, you'll learn some foundational principles of physics that will start you well on your way to knowing all about mechanical engineering.

Construct a candy machine that dispenses one candy at a time, a ball contraption that makes marbles climb stairs, a wind-up catapult, a coin bank with ramps and more.

CANDY MACHINE

Construct a candy machine that dispenses one piece of candy at a time! This is a great little contraption to keep on your desk or on the kitchen counter. Make the candy chamber taller if you'd like it to hold more candy, and be sure to use individually wrapped candy. You don't want your LEGO bricks to get sticky!

HOW IT WORKS

This machine uses a gear rack, which is basically a gear that is spread out in a line instead of having the usual round shape. A gear rack allows a machine to convert circular motion into lateral (side-to-side) motion. To be more specific, you turn the handle on the side of the candy machine, and this turns a 20-tooth bevel gear inside. The teeth of the gear connect with the gear rack, and as it turns, the gear rack slides forward, which pushes a piece of candy out of the machine. Turn the handle back again, and the gear will push the rack backward, allowing the next piece of candy to drop down. Then you can lift the handle again and dispense another piece. Such a simple mechanism and yet SO COOL!

DID YOU KNOW?

In a coin-operated candy machine, the coin becomes part of the mechanism. You insert your coin and turn the handle, and a gear turns with the coin riding along in a notch in the gear. The presence of the coin allows the gear to turn fully. Without a coin present, a sliding bar slips into the notch in the gear and prevents it from turning. No coin, no candy!

PARTS LIST

RED BRICKS
9—2 x 4 bricks
1—2 x 3 brick
3—1 x 6 bricks
4—1 x 4 bricks
2—1 x 3 bricks
3—1 x 2 bricks
1—4 x 6 plate
1—2 x 10 plate
6—2 x 6 plates
2—1 x 8 plates
2—1 x 6 plates
2—1 x 4 plates
2—Technic bushes

BLUE BRICKS
3—1 x 6 bricks
7—1 x 4 bricks
2—1 x 3 bricks
4—2 x 2 round bricks

LIGHT GRAY BRICKS
1—6 x 10 plate
1—1 x 6 plate
3—1 x 3 plates
1—1 x 3 brick
2—1 x 4 Technic bricks
3—2 x 4 tiles
1—1 x 8 tile
1—1 x 4 tile
3—1 x 3 tiles
1—Technic axle, 7 studs long
2—1 x 4 Technic gear racks
1—Technic bevel gear, 20 tooth

YELLOW BRICKS
6—1 x 6 bricks
6—1 x 1 bricks
2—1 x 4 plates
2—1 x 3 plates

ASSORTED BRICKS
4—1 x 4 x 3 clear panels
6—1 x 2 clear bricks
1—1 x 3 Technic liftarm with two
   axle holes and a pin/crank
1—8 x 16 green plate

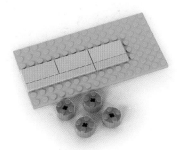

STEP 1: Attach three 2 x 4 tiles, a 1 x 8 tile and a 1 x 4 tile to an 8 x 16 plate. Find four 2 x 2 round bricks to be feet for the candy machine.

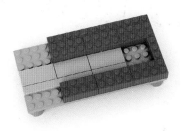

STEP 2: Add a layer of red bricks around the edge of the candy machine base.

STEP 3: Find six 2 x 6 red plates, two 1 x 6 red plates and two 1 x 3 light gray plates.

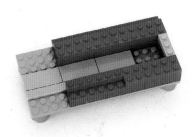

STEP 4: Stack the 2 x 6 plates in groups of two. Place two of these on the left side and one on the right. Add two 1 x 6 plates on the right side. Place two 1 x 3 light gray plates on the back of the machine.

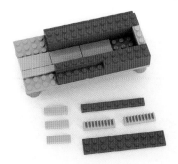

STEP 5: Gather the bricks shown for building the arm that will push the candy out.

STEP 6: Place the 1 x 8 plate next to the 2 x 10 plate. Connect them with three 1 x 3 tiles. Then attach the gear racks.

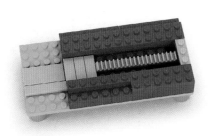  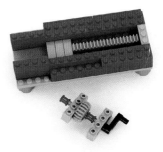

STEP 7: The gear rack arm should fit inside the candy machine. It will slide back and forth on the tiles.

STEP 8: Attach two 1 x 4 bricks on each side at the front of the candy machine. Then find two 1 x 4 Technic bricks, two Technic bushes, a 20-tooth bevel gear, an axle (7 studs long) and a 1 x 3 liftarm with a pin/crank.

STEP 9: Slide the bricks onto the axle in the order shown.

  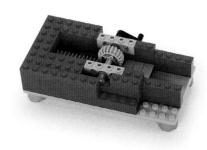

STEP 10: Attach the Technic bricks to the candy machine. Make sure that the handle is all the way to the left and that the sliding arm is as far back as it can go. If things don't line up quite right when you attach the bricks, detach them and try again.

STEP 11: Add another layer of red bricks around the edge of the machine. Bricks added are three 2 x 4 bricks, one 2 x 3 brick, one 1 x 3 brick and two 1 x 2 bricks. Then find the bricks shown.

STEP 12: Stack the bricks and plates and attach them to the side of the machine.

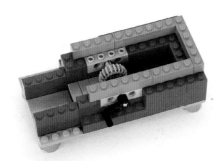 

STEP 13: Add a layer of blue bricks as shown.

STEP 14: Add a second layer of blue bricks, and then grab a 1 x 6 light gray plate and a 6 x 10 light gray plate.

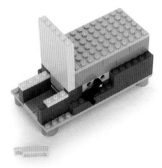

STEP 15: Cover the mechanism of the machine with the light gray plates. Build a wall for the back of the candy chamber by stacking six 1 x 6 yellow bricks. Then grab a 1 x 3 light gray brick and a 1 x 3 light gray plate.

STEP 16: Attach the 1 x 3 light gray brick and the 1 x 3 light gray plate to the bottom of the yellow wall.

STEP 17: Place the yellow wall on the body of the candy machine. Add a 1 x 4 yellow plate and a 1 x 3 yellow plate to the front of the machine. Then stack a 1 x 4 yellow plate on top of a 1 x 3 yellow plate as shown.

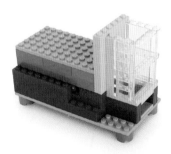

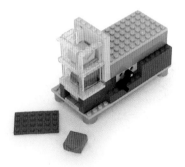

STEP 18: Attach the two yellow plates to the front of the candy machine. This creates the space where the candy will come out. Then stack six 1 x 1 yellow bricks and six 1 x 2 clear bricks. Find four 1 x 4 x 3 clear panels.

STEP 19: Build the candy chamber as shown. It's fun to see the candy in the machine, but if you don't have the clear bricks and panels, regular bricks will work just as well.

STEP 20: Fill the candy chamber with individually wrapped candies. Then grab a 4 x 6 red plate.

STEP 21: Place the 4 x 6 red plate on the top of the candy chamber, and the candy machine is complete!

To operate the machine, rotate the handle up. The arm will push a piece of candy out. Rotate the arm down again, and the next piece of candy will drop down.

COIN BANK

You'll have no trouble saving your money with this clever coin bank! Insert a coin into the slot on the side of the bank, and watch it roll down three ramps and into the storage drawer in the bottom. When you need to retrieve your money, simply pull open the drawer and take what you need. Now that's a smart way to manage your cash!

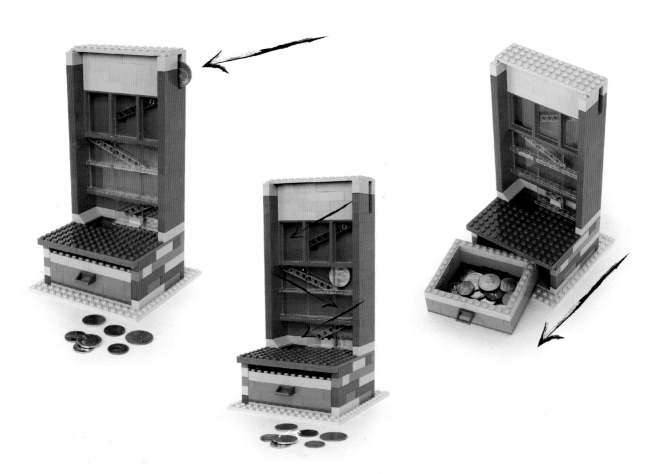

HOW IT WORKS

When you're creating contraptions with ramps and coins, you'll need to pay attention to two things: the speed of your coins and the space between the ramps. As you build, make sure that your largest coin (a quarter, for U.S. residents) will fit between your ramps as it rolls from one ramp to the next. Experiment with the tilt of your ramps as well. You want your coins to roll easily, but if your ramps are too steep, the coins will fly down to the bottom so fast that you barely have time to watch them! Use clear panels or windows to build a wall on the front. Make sure that your wall sits right up against the liftarms, and then there's no chance your coins will fall off the edge of the ramps.

PARTS LIST

DARK GRAY BRICKS
1—8 x 8 plate
1—6 x 6 plate
2—6 x 8 plates
1—4 x 8 plate
1—4 x 4 plate
1—1 x 10 plate
1—2 x 12 plate
2—2 x 4 plates
2—1 x 6 plates
2—1 x 4 plates

2—1 x 2 Technic bricks with two holes
3—1 x 2 Technic bricks
1—1 x 2 tile with handle

LIGHT GRAY BRICKS
15—2 x 4 tiles
1—2 x 4 slope
1—1 x 2 brick with two studs on the side
1—4 x 10 plate
2—2 x 4 plates
5—Technic pins

ASSORTED BRICKS
1—16 x 16 baseplate
1—tan Technic axle pin
1—1 x 7 Technic liftarm
2—1 x 9 Technic liftarms
8—1 x 4 x 3 clear panels
3—1 x 4 x 5 windows
1—1 x 10 red plate
1—1 x 2 red plate
Various light gray bricks
Various blue bricks for the drawer
Various bricks for building the body of the bank, any color

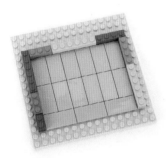

STEP 1: Grab a 16 x 16 baseplate. If you don't have this size, build your bank on a 32 x 32 baseplate. Attach fifteen 2 x 4 tiles to make the base where the drawer will sit. Substitute other sizes of tiles if you don't have enough 2 x 4 tiles. Add a row of bricks around the base.

STEP 2: Add four more layers of bricks.

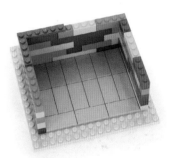

STEP 3: In the top left corner, add a 1 x 6 dark gray plate and a 1 x 4 dark gray plate.

STEP 4: Build the covering for the drawer area. Grab a 1 x 6 plate, a 6 x 6 plate, a 4 x 8 plate and an 8 x 8 plate.

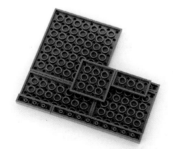

STEP 5: Attach these plates to each other by adding a 4 x 4 plate, a 2 x 4 plate, a 1 x 4 plate and a 1 x 10 plate on the underside.

STEP 6: Place this layer of plates onto the coin bank so that it lines up with the dark gray plates from step 3.

STEP 7: Add a 2 x 4 light gray slope and a layer of light gray bricks as shown.

STEP 8: Build the walls of the coin bank. As you build, add 1 x 2 Technic bricks and pins to hold the liftarms. If you position your Technic bricks on every other row as shown here, you'll need to alternate 1 x 2 Technic bricks with one hole and 1 x 2 Technic bricks with two holes to get the spacing to line up correctly. The bottom liftarm will rest on the top of the coin drawer, so you'll only need one pin for that one. The red section is 16 bricks high.

STEP 9: As you build the walls of the coin bank, leave a one-stud-wide gap on the side. This will be the slot for coins.

STEP 10: Add one layer of light gray bricks and one layer of light gray plates. This will make the coin slot three bricks plus one plate tall, which is tall enough for a quarter to fit.

STEP 11: Attach two 1 x 9 liftarms and one 1 x 7 liftarm. Place a 1 x 2 light gray brick under the bottom of the 1 x 7 liftarm. This will prop it up at the right angle so that the coins roll right into the drawer. You may want to add your liftarms as you build the walls and test the ramps as you go.

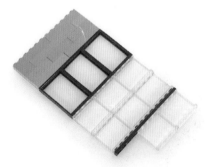

STEP 12: Design the front wall of your coin bank. Use as many clear panels or windows as you can so that you can see the coins rolling down. Then fill in the rest of the space with bricks. This wall is 18 bricks and 1 plate high.

STEP 13: Attach the front wall to the body of the coin bank.

STEP 14: Cover the top of the bank with two 2 x 4 plates and a 4 x 10 plate.

STEP 15: Build a drawer to hold the coins. Grab two 6 x 8 dark gray plates, a 2 x 12 dark gray plate and a 2 x 4 dark gray plate.

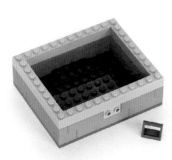

STEP 16: Build three rows of bricks around the edges. Shown are two rows of blue and one row of light gray. Place a 1 x 2 light gray brick with two studs on the side on the front of the drawer to hold the handle.

STEP 17: Attach the drawer handle, slide the drawer in place and the coin bank is complete!

Now grab some coins and test out your bank!

BALANCING NOTHING

Use your LEGO bricks to build a balance, then use it to find out how many minifigures are equal to three marbles. Or how many bricks are equal to two wheels. Once you have the hang of it, you can easily set up a fun physics trick! Use this balance to balance . . . nothing! By moving the fulcrum of your balance, you can keep one side of your balance empty and still get it to sit perfectly level by adding extra mass to the other side. Science is so cool!

HOW IT WORKS

A balance is a first-class lever. Because the two pans are an equal distance from the fulcrum in the middle, they balance when the weight on both sides is equal. When you move the fulcrum off-center, the principle of the lever comes into play. This principle states that the effort applied to a lever times its distance from the fulcrum equals the load that you are lifting times its distance from the fulcrum. In other words, when you move the fulcrum closer to one side of the balance, you'll need to reduce the mass on the other side to get the balance to . . . balance!

This project brings up an important science concept: mass versus weight. When we talk about how heavy something is, we usually talk about its weight. However, weight is a measure of how much gravity pulls on an object, whereas mass refers to the amount of matter, or "stuff," in an object. If you traveled to the moon, you would have the same mass as you do here on earth. However, your weight would be less because the force of gravity is weaker on the moon. You'll hear the word "mass" more often in science books, because it's a more specific term for talking about how heavy something is.

PARTS LIST

BLUE BRICKS
12—1 x 6 bricks
4—1 x 4 bricks
4—1 x 2 bricks

ASSORTED BRICKS
1—16 x 16 plate (or smaller)
4—4 x 6 red plates
2—1 x 16 dark gray Technic bricks
9—2 x 4 green bricks
2—1 x 4 green bricks
2—2 x 4 green plates
1—2 x 2 light gray brick with a pin on
   each side

STEP 1: Let's start with a basic balance, but we'll be making it kind of crazy in a minute! Build the pans for the balance. Attach two 4 x 6 red plates by building a perimeter of blue bricks (two bricks high).

STEP 2: Build the frame for the balance. Stack nine 2 x 4 bricks. Then add a 2 x 2 brick with two pins at the top.

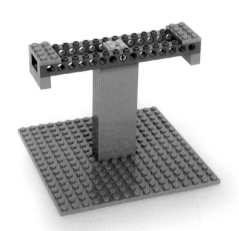

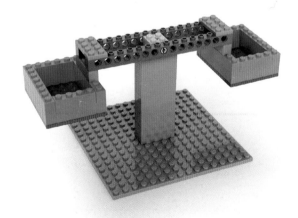

STEP 3: Attach the two 1 x 16 Technic bricks to the pins. Place a 2 x 4 plate and a 1 x 4 brick on each end as shown.

STEP 4: Attach the pans on each side and check to make sure that your balance sits level. If it's lopsided, double-check your bricks to make sure that you used exactly the same number of bricks (and the same sizes) on each side.

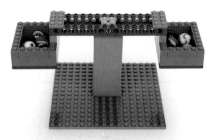

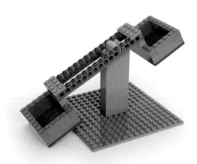

STEP 5: Now it's time to experiment! Test out your balance with some marbles, or another object. It should balance when the mass of the contents of the pans are equal.

STEP 6: Now try moving the fulcrum. Attach the Technic bricks so that the pins are on the fourth holes from the ends. Whoa! That's a little crazy!

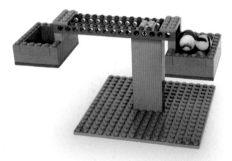

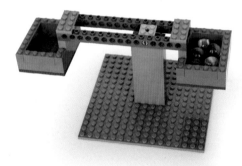

STEP 7: How many marbles does it take to make the sides balance? This photo shows eight marbles on one side to balance nothing on the other side.

STEP 8: Move the fulcrum over one hole closer to the center. Before you fill up the pan with marbles, guess how many it will take to balance this time.

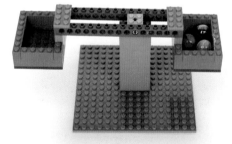

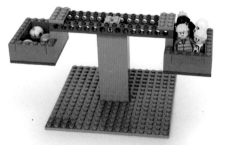

STEP 9: Continue moving the fulcrum one hole closer to the center. With the marbles pictured, it took 8 to balance, then 5, then 3.

Move the fulcrum back to the center and keep experimenting with your balance. Here are some ideas to get you started! How many minifigures are equal to the mass of three marbles? How many bricks are equal to the mass of one large wheel? Which has more mass—a 2 x 4 brick, or three 2 x 4 plates stacked on top of each other? (They take up the same amount of space, but try it and see!)

WIND-UP CATAPULT

Launch mini projectiles into the air with this powerful little catapult. In this design, a rubber band creates tension on the arm of the catapult. Wind up the rubber band by turning the gear. When you think that you have wound it up enough, pull out the axle and watch the ball fly!

HOW IT WORKS

Winding up the catapult creates stored energy, called potential energy, in the rubber band. The more tension the rubber band has, the greater its potential energy. When you remove the axle, the arm of the catapult is free to move, and all that potential energy is converted to kinetic energy, or the energy of motion, as the rubber band pulls down on the arm.

This catapult has another cool feature as well—a ratchet system. A ratchet is a device that allows a wheel to turn in one direction, but stops it from turning back the other direction. It consists of a gear and a pawl. The pawl is a rod that sits between the teeth of the gear. When you wind up the catapult, the gear will naturally try to turn back the other direction because of the tension of the rubber band. The pawl makes contact between the teeth of the gear and prevents it from turning. Without the ratchet, it would be much harder to wind up the catapult!

PARTS LIST

TAN BRICKS
8—2 x 6 bricks
2—2 x 4 bricks
6—1 x 4 bricks
4—2 x 2 bricks
4—1 x 2 bricks
2—1 x 3 bricks
2—1 x 4 Technic bricks
1—Technic axle pin without friction ridges

BROWN BRICKS
4—2 x 8 plates
4—2 x 6 plates

2—1 x 4 Technic bricks
1—2 x 4 brick
1—1 x 2 brick
1—1 x 1 brick
1—1 x 1 brick with a handle on the side
2—2 x 2 round bricks

LIGHT GRAY BRICKS
1—6 x 10 plate
2—4 x 10 plates
2—2 x 4 plates
1—Technic axle, 3 studs long
1—Technic axle, 5 studs long
1—Technic axle, 9 studs long
1—1 x 2 Technic brick

4—Technic bushes
1—Technic pin
1—wheel with an axle hole

ASSORTED BRICKS
8—2 x 4 dark azure bricks
1—Technic gear, 24 tooth
1—2 x 2 dark gray round tile with a hole
1—black Technic axle, 10 studs long
1—black Technic connector #1
2—1 x 16 dark gray Technic bricks

OTHER ITEMS
1—rubber band
1—plastic LEGO ball

STEP 1: Build the base of the catapult. Grab a 6 x 10 plate and two 4 x 10 plates. Connect the 4 x 10 plates to each other with two 2 x 4 plates.

STEP 2: Add a row of 2 x 4 bricks on each side of the base.

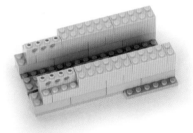

STEP 3: Build two layers of tan bricks on each side. Place a 1 x 4 Technic brick on both sides of the front end.

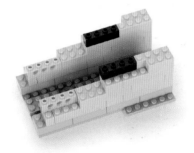

STEP 4: On each side, add a 2 x 6 brick and a 2 x 2 brick. On top of those, add a 1 x 4 brick, a 1 x 3 brick and a 1 x 4 Technic brick on each side.

STEP 5: Gather the bricks shown for building the shooting arm.

STEP 6: Use two 2 x 8 plates to connect the two 1 x 16 Technic bricks. Build a bucket for the projectile with two 2 x 6 plates and four 1 x 4 bricks.

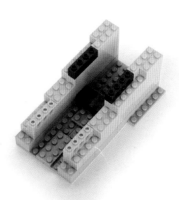

STEP 7: Slide the axle (9 studs long) through the fifth hole in the Technic bricks and add the two Technic bushes.

STEP 8: Place a 2 x 4 brick in the bottom of the catapult. This will keep the shooting arm from swinging too far.

STEP 9: Slide the axle (9 studs long) through the Technic bricks on each side. (You'll need to briefly remove the Technic bricks.) Then add a second Technic bush on each side to hold the axle in place. Check to make sure the connection is still loose enough that the arm can rotate freely.

STEP 10: Grab a black axle (10 studs long) and a wheel with an axle hole.

STEP 11: Slide the axle (10 studs long) through the first hole on each brown Technic brick. Then add the wheel with an axle hole to the end of the axle. This will prevent the shooting arm from moving until you are ready to launch.

STEP 12: Gather the bricks shown for building the wind-up mechanism.

STEP 13: Attach the round bricks to either side of the 1 x 2 brick, 1 x 1 brick and 1 x 1 brick with a handle.

STEP 14: Attach the 2 x 2 round tile with a hole to the side that has studs showing on the end and add the light gray Technic axle (3 studs long) to that side. Slide another light gray axle (5 studs long) into the round brick on the other side.

STEP 15: Slide the wind-up assembly into the first hole in the Technic bricks on the front of the catapult. Slide a 24-tooth gear onto the axle (5 studs long). Then gather the bricks shown.

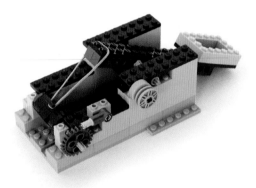

STEP 16: Attach the Technic connector #1 to a gray pin that has been inserted into a 1 x 2 Technic brick. Slide the axle pin into the end of the Technic connector. The tan pin can move upward freely if you lift it. However, gravity keeps it sitting on the teeth of the gear, which prevents the gear from turning backward. Stretch a rubber band around the brown handle and around the shooting arm. Your catapult is now ready to go!

BUILDING TIP

You may want to experiment with different rubber bands to find just the right one. You'll want to choose a rubber band that is thick enough to provide good torque (force that causes something to twist) but not so thick that it pulls the catapult apart.

Grab a plastic LEGO ball or something similar and test your catapult. Be careful to use lightweight objects as projectiles and not marbles or anything that might injure someone.

SPEEDY SPINNER

This little gadget demonstrates the effect of changing gear sizes in a hilarious way! Turn the handle slowly, and the minifigure on the right will spin quickly—as in, NINE times as fast. Rotate the handle as fast as you can, and the minifigure on the right side might even fly off! Once you have built your spinning contraption, try modifying it to make a personal fan. Or add a propeller and watch a cool demonstration of inertia.

HOW IT WORKS

It's easy to see how gears work by looking at them—the teeth mesh together so that when you turn one gear, it causes the one meshed with it to turn also, but in the opposite direction. But what happens when you combine gears of different sizes? This project uses 24-tooth gears and 8-tooth gears. When a 24-tooth gear is turning an 8-tooth gear, the 8-tooth gear will rotate three complete turns in the amount of time it takes the 24-tooth gear to turn once. It's a ratio of 3 to 1—24 divided by 8 is 3, so the 8-tooth gear will rotate 3 times as fast as the 24-tooth gear. In this project, you will speed up the rotation by a total of 9 times. The first 8-tooth gear will "gear up" the machine 3 times. Adding a second 8-tooth gear will speed it up again by 3 times, making the final rotation 9 times as fast. Wow, that's fast!

PARTS LIST

LIGHT GRAY BRICKS
1—6 x 10 plate
2—1 x 2—2 x 2 brackets, inverted
2—Technic axles, 7 studs long
1—Technic axle, 5 studs long
4—Technic bushes
1—1 x 3 Technic liftarm with two axle
   holes and a pin/crank

DARK GRAY BRICKS
2—Technic gears, 24 tooth
2—Technic gears, 8 tooth
1—2 x 10 brick
1—2 x 6 brick
7—2 x 4 bricks
1—2 x 2 brick

RED BRICKS
4—1 x 4 bricks
1—Technic bush
2—1 x 8 Technic bricks

ASSORTED BRICKS
2—2 x 2 yellow round bricks
1—2 x 2 blue brick with a pin on top
1—4-blade propeller

STEP 1: Attach four 1 x 4 red bricks to a light gray 6 x 10 plate.

STEP 2: Slide a 24-tooth gear and two Technic bushes onto an axle (7 studs long). Then slide an 8-tooth gear, a 24-tooth gear and a Technic bush onto an axle (5 studs long). Slide a Technic bush, then an 8-tooth gear, then another Technic bush onto an axle (7 studs long).

STEP 3: Slide the axles into the second, fourth and sixth holes on a 1 x 8 Technic brick.

STEP 4: Add another 1 x 8 Technic brick at the top. Then attach the two Technic bricks to the red bricks from step 1. Gather the other bricks shown.

STEP 5: Attach a 2 x 2 yellow round brick to the end of both axles. Attach the handle to the bottom of the axle on the left side. Then build a base to hold the spinner. Add two 1 x 2—2 x 2 inverted brackets.

STEP 6: Attach the spinner to the base by using the brackets. Add some minifigures and give them a ride!

Now try something different with your spinner. Take off the minifigures and add a 2 x 2 brick with a pin on top. Attach a 4-blade propeller to the pin.

Spin the spinner and get the propeller spinning super fast. What happens when you stop turning the handle? The propeller keeps spinning for several seconds! Why does this happen? The propeller spins easily because there is very little friction between it and the blue pin. Once you get it spinning, it will keep spinning unless it's acted on by an outside force. The force could be your hand stopping it, or it will stop eventually because of the force of friction—the propeller and the pin do rub together, and this will eventually cause it to slow down and stop.

Try turning your spinner into a little personal fan! Experiment with different sized blades and see which works the best. You'll notice that as your blades get bigger, they move more air, which could possibly make a better fan. But the bigger blades also experience more air resistance, which means that you have to use more force to turn the handle. Try to find the best size and shape for the blades that gives you the most effective fan.

DID YOU KNOW?

The famous scientist Sir Isaac Newton discovered that an object in motion tends to stay in motion unless acted on by an outside force, and an object at rest tends to stay at rest unless acted on by an outside force. This principle is described in his first law of motion, and the name for this is inertia.

BALL STAIRS CIRCUIT

Turn the handle on this contraption, and a ball climbs a set of stairs, rolls down a ramp and then gets back in line and does it again! It's totally mesmerizing to watch, and your friends and family will be completely impressed. If you don't have all the bricks needed for building the mechanism, you'll definitely want to consider ordering them because this is an epic project. Note that the pictures show LEGO plastic balls, but marbles work just as well.

HOW IT WORKS

This project uses a crankshaft and pistons to create the up-and-down motion of the stairs. A crankshaft is an axle with 90-degree bends in it. When you turn the crank, the shape of the crank shaft causes the pistons to go up and down. See step 11 for a visual explanation of the crankshaft.

The motion of the stairs causes the ball to climb. When one stair is at its highest position, the next stair has dropped to its lowest position, so the ball easily rolls down to the next stair. The 1 x 2 plates on the front end of each stair keep the ball heading in the right direction.

TROUBLESHOOTING

The stairs can get caught on each other if any pieces are out of alignment. If your stairs get stuck, try pressing down each brick to make sure that it is solidly in place. You may need to take the stairs off and reattach them to ensure that they are attached tightly. Also check for any bricks that have dents or scratches as those can also keep the bricks from moving smoothly past each other.

PARTS LIST

RED BRICKS
8—2 x 8 bricks
17—2 x 4 bricks
17—2 x 2 bricks
1—2 x 3 brick
5—1 x 2 bricks
5—2 x 2 plates

BLUE BRICKS
2—2 x 6 bricks
15—2 x 4 bricks
6—2 x 3 bricks
24—2 x 2 bricks
3—1 x 6 bricks
12—1 x 4 bricks
3—1 x 3 bricks
1—1 x 2 Technic brick
1—1 x 1 brick
1—2 x 2 plate
1—1 x 4 plate

TAN BRICKS
1—16 x 16 baseplate
3—2 x 4 tiles
3—1 x 4 tiles
2—2 x 2 tiles
5—1 x 2 tiles
2—2 x 2 curved slopes
1—1 x 3 curved slope
1—2 x 2 plate
1—1 x 1 tile

DARK GRAY BRICKS
1—4 x 10 plate
1—4 x 8 plate
1—4 x 6 plate
1—2 x 4 plate
7—1 x 2 Technic bricks
10—Technic connectors #1

LIGHT GRAY BRICKS
8—Technic pins
10—axles, 3 studs long
1—1 x 4 Technic brick
6—Technic axle and pin connectors, perpendicular, 3 studs long with a center pin hole
1—1 x 2 Technic liftarm with a pin hole and an axle hole, thick

ASSORTED BRICKS
2—1 x 2 brown (or any color) Technic bricks
5—1 x 2 light blue plates
1—black axle, 4 studs long
2—1 x 2 black Technic liftarms, thin
2—red Technic axles, 2 studs long with notches
1—hinge brick
1—1 x 3 black Technic liftarm with two axle holes and pin/crank

STEP 1: Build two layers of bricks in the shape shown. Use blue bricks, or substitute any color.

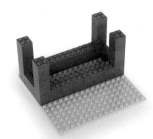

STEP 2: Add a stack of five 2 x 2 bricks to each corner.

STEP 3: Find a 1 x 2 Technic brick, a gray pin, a 1 x 2 liftarm with a pin hole and an axle hole, a red axle (2 studs long with notches) and an axle and pin connector (perpendicular, 3 studs long with a center pin hole).

STEP 4: Use the gray pin to connect the liftarm and Technic brick. Then insert the red axle.

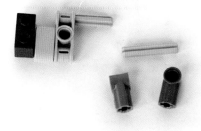

STEP 5: Attach the Technic axle and pin connector to the other end of the red Technic axle (2 studs long with notches). Then add an axle (3 studs long). Find another axle (3 studs long) and two Technic connectors #1.

STEP 6: Put a connector #1 on each end of the axle (3 studs long). Then slide this onto the mechanism as shown.

CURIOUS CONTRAPTIONS

STEP 7: Add another axle and pin connector, then another set of #1 connectors with an axle in between, and so on, following the pattern shown.

STEP 8: Find the bricks shown. The black axle is 4 studs long, and the two black liftarms are thin 1 x 2s with two axle holes.

STEP 9: Slide the handle, Technic brick and two black liftarms onto the black axle. Then slide the red axle into the black liftarms.

STEP 10: Add a 1 x 2 dark gray Technic brick to the right side of each piston by attaching it with a gray pin.

STEP 11: The crankshaft and pistons are now complete. Check to be sure that your mechanism looks exactly like this before moving on!

STEP 12: Build the stairs. Each stair has a 1 x 2 red brick on the bottom. From left to right, here's what you should add on top of the 1 x 2 brick. Stair 1 is four 2 x 2 bricks and two 2 x 2 plates. Stair 2 is four 2 x 2 bricks. Stair 3 is three 2 x 2 bricks and one 2 x 2 plate. Stair 4 is two 2 x 2 bricks and two 2 x 2 plates. Stair 5 is two 2 x 2 bricks.

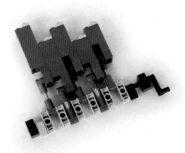

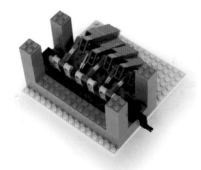

STEP 13: Attach the stairs to the 1 x 2 dark gray Technic bricks from step 10.

STEP 14: Attach the mechanism to the frame of the machine. The brown Technic bricks should be centered on each side.

STEP 15: Build this shape with two layers of red bricks (or bricks of any color).

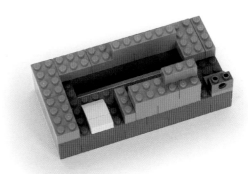

STEP 16: Add a layer of blue bricks. On the front right corner, add a 2 x 2 blue plate and a 1 x 2 dark gray Technic brick. Place a 2 x 2 tan plate on the frame three studs from the left side. Then find the bricks shown.

STEP 17: Add the blue bricks to the frame as shown. Place the 1 x 2 tan tile and the 2 x 2 tan curved slope on top of the 2 x 2 tan plate. The curved slope should slope toward the back of the frame.

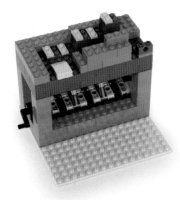

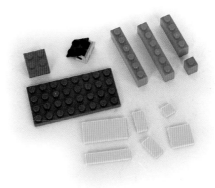

STEP 18: This is the hardest step! Attach the top of the frame to the rest of the machine. The tricky part is holding up all the stairs while you attach the top of the frame. One option is to turn the whole thing upside down while you attach it. This will keep the stairs in the correct position. Another option is to remove the stairs and attach them one at a time after you attach the top section of the frame.

STEP 19: Grab the bricks shown for building the ramp.

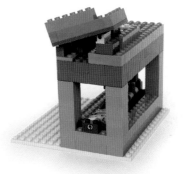

STEP 20: Attach the bricks and tiles to the 4 x 8 plate. Attach the hinge brick to the 2 x 2 red brick.

STEP 21: Now attach the ramp to the hinge brick, and then add it to the machine.

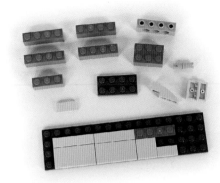

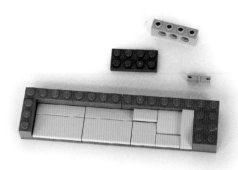

STEP 22: Build the second ramp. Attach tan tiles and a 1 x 4 blue plate to a 4 x 10 plate and a 4 x 6 plate as shown. Then gather the bricks shown.

STEP 23: Attach the blue bricks on the perimeter of the ramp. Place the 1 x 2 tan tile and the 2 x 2 curved slope on top of the 1 x 4 blue plate. Then add the 1 x 3 tan curved slope in the corner.

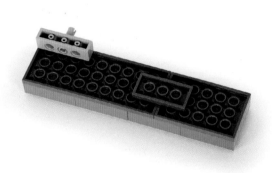

STEP 24: Turn the ramp upside down. Add a 2 x 4 plate for support. Then attach a 1 x 4 Technic brick with a gray pin in the center hole.

STEP 25: Build a tower of eight 2 x 4 bricks to support the ramp. Place a 1 x 2 Technic brick on top and insert a gray pin. Then add a 1 x 2 dark gray Technic brick to the underside of the ramp.

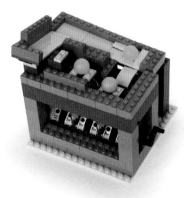

STEP 26: Attach the ramp to the support tower. Then attach it to the ball circuit as shown.

Now it's time to play! Grab some marbles or LEGO balls and start turning the crank!

MARBLE SPIRAL

Use your bricks to build a tower with a spiral of ramps inside. Drop a marble in the top, and it will roll around the spiral and pop out through the exit at the bottom. Use as many clear bricks, panels or windows in your construction as you can so that you can watch the marble travel down. Then use your marble spiral as a component in a fun chain reaction!

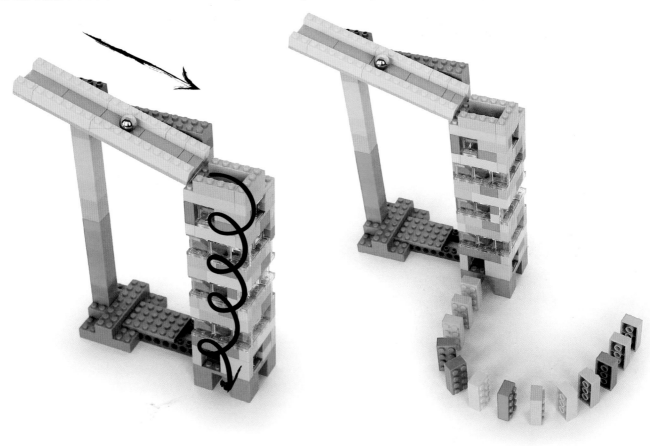

HOW IT WORKS

Did you know that a ramp is a machine? It's called an inclined plane, and it makes it easier to either lift or lower objects. In this contraption, a series of ramps turned at 90-degree angles creates a spiral for a marble to roll down.

Use your marble spiral as a component in a chain reaction! The marble will roll down the ramp, through the spiral and then set off a chain of falling 2 x 4 bricks. The scientific term for what's happening is "a transfer of energy." The rolling ball has kinetic energy, or the energy of motion, and when it bumps the first 2 x 4 brick, it transfers its energy to the brick. The falling brick then transfers energy to each brick in the series.

BUILDING TIPS

If you don't have all the bricks pictured, you can build a shorter spiral that will work just as well. This will also reduce the number of bricks needed for the ramp frame.

You'll need to find a small marble or steel ball bearing (½-inch [13-mm] size) for this project. Most glass marbles will get stuck in the spiral.

DID YOU KNOW?

You may have heard of Rube Goldberg machines—crazy contraptions in which a very simple task, such as turning off a light switch, is accomplished in a totally zany way through a series of cause-and-effect actions. But did you know that Rube Goldberg (1883–1970) was a Pulitzer Prize–winning cartoonist? The concept of the Rube Goldberg machine comes from Goldberg's hilarious cartoons about the fictitious Professor Butts and his elaborate inventions.

PARTS LIST

SPIRAL
16—2 x 3 slopes
1—6 x 6 plate
8—2 x 2 bricks
30—1 x 2 x 2 clear panels
1—2 x 6 plate
1—2 x 2 tile
Various bricks, 1 stud wide

RAMP AND FRAME
4—1 x 14 Technic bricks
2—1 x 6 Technic bricks
4—2 x 4 bricks
3—2 x 6 bricks
1—2 x 8 brick
1—4 x 6 plate
1—4 x 10 plate
1—4 x 8 plate
1—2 x 10 plate
4—2 x 4 tiles
2—1 x 2 tiles

2—1 x 6 bricks
2—1 x 8 bricks
1—1 x 2 Technic brick
36—2 x 2 bricks
1—light gray pin
1—light gray pin, 3 studs long
2 x 4 bricks to use as dominoes

OTHER ITEMS
Small marbles or steel ball bearings—pictured are ½-inch (13-mm) steel balls

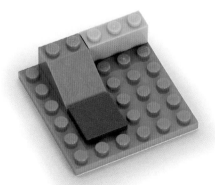

STEP 1: Start building your spiral with a 6 x 6 plate. Attach a 2 x 2 tile, a 2 x 3 slope and a 1 x 3 brick as shown.

STEP 2: Add a 1 x 3 brick, a 1 x 2 brick and a 1 x 2 x 2 clear panel. If you don't have clear panels, substitute a window or simply use more bricks.

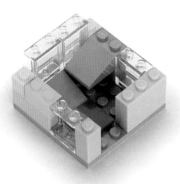

STEP 3: Add (from left to right) two 1 x 1 bricks (stacked), a 1 x 2 brick, a 1 x 1 brick, two clear panels, a 1 x 1 brick, a 2 x 3 slope, a clear panel and two 1 x 3 bricks.

STEP 4: Continue the spiral by attaching a 1 x 4 brick, a 1 x 2 brick and another 2 x 3 slope. Are you starting to see the pattern of the slope bricks? Each one is placed one brick higher and 90 degrees to the right.

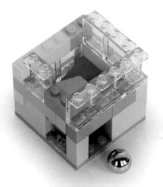

STEP 5: Leave an opening for the marble to exit the spiral and place a 1 x 3 brick above the opening. Then add a 1 x 1 brick and a 1 x 4 brick.

STEP 6: Add the next 2 x 3 brick. Then add a row of clear panels or bricks. Test out your ramp! Can you start a marble from the highest blue slope and have it come out the exit?

STEP 7: Place the next 2 x 3 slope on the spiral and fill in with bricks.

STEP 8: Just keep building, following the pattern!

STEP 9: Close up the top by adding a 2 x 6 plate, a 1 x 6 brick, two 1 x 3 bricks and a 1 x 4 brick.

STEP 10: Now build a frame so that you can construct a ramp leading to your marble spiral. Connect two 1 x 14 Technic bricks with two 2 x 4 bricks. Add towers built from 2 x 2 bricks, or build a solid wall if you prefer.

STEP 11: Reinforce the base with a 4 x 6 plate, two 2 x 6 bricks and a 2 x 8 brick. Or figure out your own method!

STEP 12: Grab the bricks shown for building the supports for the ramp.

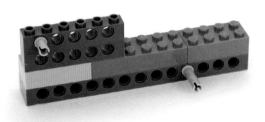

STEP 13: Place the 2 x 4 bricks and the 2 x 6 brick on top of both 1 x 14 Technic bricks. Then add the two 1 x 6 Technic bricks. Insert the pins as shown.

STEP 14: Attach the ramp supports to the top of your frame.

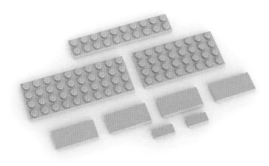

STEP 15: Gather the bricks shown for building the ramp.

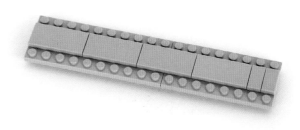

STEP 16: Use the 2 x 10 plate to attach the 4 x 10 plate and the 4 x 8 plate. Then add tiles in the center.

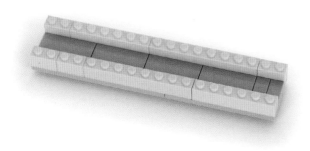

STEP 17: Add a row of bricks on each side of the ramp.

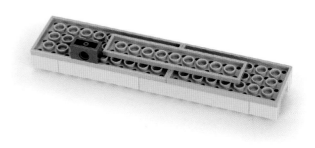

STEP 18: Turn the ramp upside down and attach a 1 x 2 Technic brick.

STEP 19: Use the 1 x 2 Technic brick from step 18 to attach the ramp to the light gray pin on the left side of the frame. The ramp rests on the longer light gray pin on the right side. Build feet on the marble spiral by adding two 2 x 2 bricks to each corner. This will position the opening at the right height for the marble to knock down a series of bricks as it exits the spiral.

Now it's time to test out your ramp and marble spiral! Once it's working well, build a chain of bricks or dominoes for your marble to knock down. What else can you add? You may even want to try creating a Rube Goldberg machine in which one motion causes another and a simple task is accomplished in a very silly and roundabout way. Maybe the final domino can ring a bell or bump a car and make it roll down a ramp!

CRAZY MARBLE SORTING CONTRAPTION

Here's another fun project with marbles! This project is similar to the classic game show game Plinko. Build a ramp and a marble maze that sorts marbles completely by chance. It's quite entertaining to watch! Choose how you'll space the pins on your marble contraption, and then watch the marbles bounce through the maze and land at the bottom. Can you predict which box the marble will fall into? Or, which box do you think will catch the most marbles? Note that if you're running low on bricks, this game will work just as well if you make it narrower.

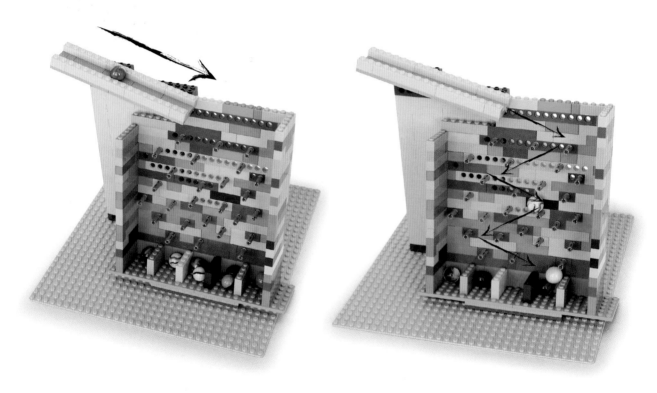

HOW IT WORKS

When a project has factors that can change, scientists refer to them as variables. There are a few variables that affect the marble's path down to the bottom in this project. Gravity is acting on the marble and pulling it down to the bottom. The marble's speed as it leaves the ramp determines how far it will travel horizontally before falling. The marble also changes direction as it hits the pins, and it loses some of its speed as well. Which pin the marble hits first will determine which pins it hits next, and the angle at which it hits the pin also makes a difference. Did the marble hit a pin with enough speed to bounce? That will affect where it goes next! Physics can be a little complicated, but thankfully it can also be super fun!

PARTS LIST

RAMP

1—32 x 32 baseplate
Various bricks, 2 studs wide, any color
2—1 x 14 dark gray Technic bricks
2—1 x 6 dark gray Technic bricks

1—light gray pin
1—light gray pin, 3 studs long
Ramp assembly from the Marble
Spiral (page 107)

MARBLE SORTING MAZE

2—6 x 12 bright green plates
2—2 x 12 plates, any color

8 or so 1 x 2 Technic bricks
Technic bricks of any length
20 or more blue pins, 3 studs long
with friction ridges
Various bricks, 1 stud wide, any color

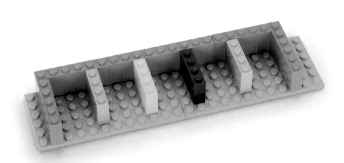

STEP 1: Start building your marble maze by creating a row of compartments at the bottom. Each space is 3 studs wide. Make the outside edges 6 studs long.

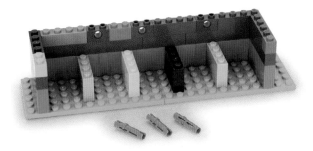

STEP 2: Add two more rows of bricks and include three 1 x 2 Technic bricks. Insert pins (3 studs long) in the holes.

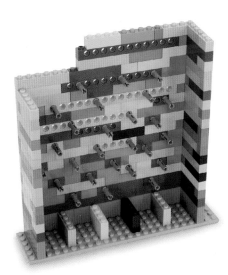

STEP 3: Keep building your maze. As you go, create places to insert more blue pins and check to be sure that the marbles you're using won't get stuck between pins. Build the walls three studs higher on the right side. The ramp will fill the space on the left.

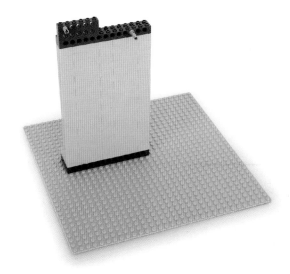

STEP 4: Build a wall to hold up the marble ramp. At the top, add two 1 x 14 Technic bricks. Then stack two 1 x 6 Technic bricks and place them on top. Insert a gray pin on the top left side and add a gray pin (3 studs long) on the right side, three studs over. The ramp will connect to the pin on the top left and will rest on top of the longer pin.

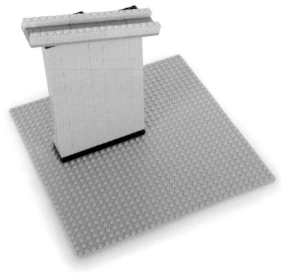

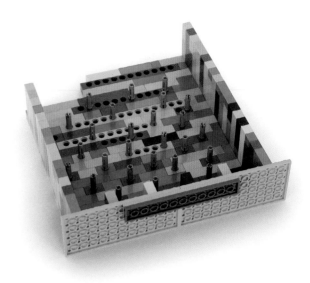

STEP 5: Build the ramp according to the directions for the Marble Spiral (page 107), and then attach it to the pins.

STEP 6: The marble maze needs to tilt a little to keep the marbles from falling out of the game as they travel down to the bottom. Place two 2 x 12 plates under the front of the maze.

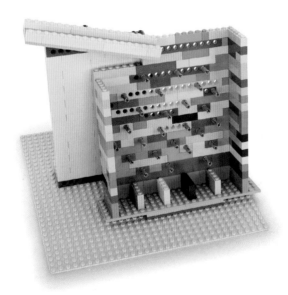

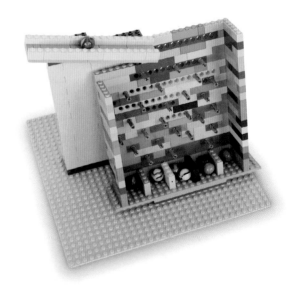

STEP 7: Place the marble maze on the baseplate so that it's leaning on the wall supporting the ramp. Your marble sorting maze is complete!

Now it's time to grab some marbles and test it out. Get a bunch, because everyone in the house is going to want a turn!

LONG-DISTANCE RACE CAR

Imagine a LEGO car rolling down a ramp. What can you do to the car to make it roll as far as possible? You could change the tires. Thick tires with sticky tread will cause more friction and slow the car down more than narrow, smooth tires will. You can also change the weight of the car. Which will roll farther, a heavy car or a light car? This project will provide you with a fun way to find out!

Use a board or something similar to create a ramp for testing how far your car will travel. The longer and steeper your ramp is, the more difference you'll notice in the performance of the empty car versus the car with added weight. Use a ruler to measure the distance that your car travels beyond the ramp.

HOW IT WORKS

All objects resist changes to their speed, and this resistance is called inertia. It takes force to overcome that resistance and make an object start moving, and it also takes force to make it stop moving. Imagine an empty toy wagon rolling down a hill. It might take a little effort, but you could probably stop it from rolling. Now imagine a hippopotamus on roller skates rolling down a hill. Do you think you would have enough force to stop the hippopotamus? Definitely not! The more mass an object has, the more it resists a change in motion.

When we are talking about the energy of moving objects, we use the word "momentum." The amount of momentum an object has is equal to its mass times its speed. So unless that wagon was rolling at lightning speed, the hippo would definitely have more momentum and require more force to stop.

Now back to our LEGO race car. Which car will gain more momentum as it rolls down the ramp—the empty car, or the car with added weight? Adding quarters will give the car more mass, and it will take more force to stop it from rolling. Thus, the heavy car will travel farther than the empty car.

PARTS LIST

LIGHT GRAY BRICKS
1—4 x 10 plate
1—4 x 4 plate
2—1 x 4 Technic bricks
2—1 x 3 bricks
1—1 x 2 x 1 panel
1—2 x 2 curved slope

RED BRICKS
1—2 x 4 plate
3—1 x 4 bricks

3—1 x 4 plates
1—2 x 6 plate
4—Technic bushes

YELLOW BRICKS
2—1 x 4 Technic bricks
1—1 x 4 brick
2—1 x 2 bricks
1—1 x 4 plate
1—2 x 4 brick, modified with curved top
2—2 x 4 plates
1—4 x 4 wedge plate

ASSORTED BRICKS
2—1 x 2 medium azure bricks
2—1 x 2 medium azure curved slopes
2—1 x 4 white plates
1—1 x 2 white plate
4—wedge belt wheels with tires
2—black Technic axles, 8 studs long
1—steering wheel

STEP 1: Connect a 4 x 4 light gray plate and a 4 x 10 light gray plate with a 2 x 4 red plate.

STEP 2: Add two 1 x 4 light gray Technic bricks so that they hang off the end by one stud. Then add two 1 x 4 yellow Technic bricks and a 1 x 4 red brick.

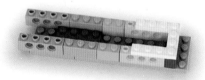

STEP 3: Fill in the sides with two 1 x 3 light gray bricks and two 1 x 2 medium azure bricks. Then add three 1 x 4 white plates to the front of the car.

STEP 4: Attach a 4 x 4 yellow wedge plate to the white plates. Then add two 1 x 2 yellow bricks, two 1 x 4 red bricks and a 1 x 4 yellow brick. Gather the bricks shown.

STEP 5: Place a 1 x 4 red plate on the front of the car and one on top of the yellow brick at the back of the car.

STEP 6: Attach the final 1 x 4 red plate and two light gray panels to the 2 x 6 red plate.

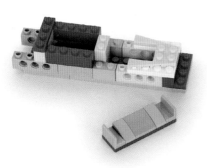

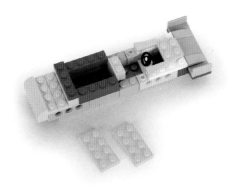

STEP 7: Add the 1 x 2 medium azure curved slopes and the 2 x 2 light gray curved slope.

STEP 8: Attach the front bumper to the car. Then add a 1 x 4 yellow plate and a 2 x 4 modified yellow brick with a curved top to the back of the car. Find two 2 x 4 yellow plates.

STEP 9: Place the two 2 x 4 yellow plates on the back of the body. Then find four wedge belt wheels, two axles (8 studs long) and four Technic bushes to hold the wheels in place.

STEP 10: Slide the axles through the Technic bricks. Then add a Technic bush on each side. Finally, add the wheels. The car is complete!

Now add some weight to the car. Quarters fit into the space perfectly, but you can also try pennies or marbles or any other small but heavy object. Then it's time to test your car! Set up a ramp and see how far it will roll. Remember that momentum also depends on an object's speed. Try increasing the slant of your ramp or making your ramp longer to increase the speed of the car. Does it roll farther before stopping? Which makes the biggest difference?

AMAZING BALANCING BIRD

Have you ever played with one of those toy birds that balances right on your finger using just its beak? Build your own LEGO version of this classic toy! The key to success is getting the center of gravity in just the right spot. Your completed bird will balance on your finger, or you can construct a base on which to display it. This bird is designed to look like an eagle, but if you prefer you can substitute bricks in any color to create your own type of bird.

HOW IT WORKS

Getting this bird to balance on its head involves building it so that its center of gravity, or balance point, is in its head. To understand the concept of balance point, try balancing a pen on your finger. The balance point might be in the center, but if your pen has a cap that adds weight to one end, the balance point will be a little closer to that end. In order for the bird to balance on its head, you must compensate for the weight in the body of the bird by adding weight to the wings and positioning them so that they are past the head.

You may have noticed that three 2 x 4 plates stacked on top of each other are equal in size to one 2 x 4 brick. However, the three plates have more mass than a 2 x 4 brick. This bird is designed with four 2 x 4 plates at the tips of its wings to add weight in just the right spots.

PARTS LIST

BROWN BRICKS
2—2 x 6 plates
8—2 x 4 plates
5—2 x 3 plates
2—2 x 2 plates
2—1 x 2 plates
3—1 x 2 plates with one stud on top
1—1 x 4 plate
1—2 x 4 wedge plate, right
1—2 x 4 wedge plate, left

1—4 x 4 wedge plate, cut corner
2—3 x 3 round corner plates
1—2 x 4 brick
1—1 x 4 brick
1—2 x 2 inverted slope
1—1 x 2 inverted slope

WHITE BRICKS
2—2 x 3 plates
5—1 x 3 plates
4—1 x 1 slopes, 30 degree

ASSORTED BRICKS
2—3 x 8 dark tan wedge plates, right
2—3 x 8 dark tan wedge plates, left
2—3 x 3 dark red wedge plates, cut corners
2—1 x 1 black round plates
1—1 x 1 yellow plate with a vertical tooth
Various dark gray bricks for building a base

STEP 1: Line up a 2 x 3 white plate and three 2 x 3 brown plates.

STEP 2: Connect the plates with two 1 x 3 white plates, a 2 x 4 brown brick, a 1 x 4 brown brick, a 2 x 2 brown inverted slope and a 1 x 2 brown inverted slope.

STEP 3: Attach the 1 x 1 yellow plate with a vertical tooth to be the beak. Then add a 2 x 3 white plate and a 1 x 3 white plate.

STEP 4: Add a 1 x 3 white plate to the head and two 1 x 1 black round plates as eyes. Then add four 1 x 1 white slopes (30 degree) and gather the bricks shown.

STEP 5: Place the final 1 x 3 white plate on top of the eyes. Then add the brown plates to the bird's back as shown. Attach the tail to the 1 x 2 plate with one stud on top.

STEP 6: Gather the bricks shown for building the right wing. Substitute with different colors if you need to.

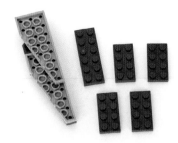

STEP 7: Connect the two 3 x 8 wedge plates so that there are four rows of studs showing at the top.

STEP 8: Then attach the rest of the plates as shown.

STEP 9: Turn the wing upside down. Find a 2 x 6 brown plate and four 2 x 4 brown plates.

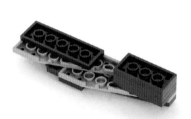

STEP 10: Stack the four 2 x 4 plates and attach them to the underside of the wing. Then add the 2 x 6 plate.

STEP 11: Build a second wing that is a mirror image of the first wing.

STEP 12: Attach the wings using the 1 x 2 plates with one stud on top. This will allow you to rotate the wings to just the right position for the bird to balance, but it's not very stable. This design works well for displaying the bird. If you want to carry the bird around to play with, attach the wings with 1 x 2 regular plates. They will need to stick straight out to the sides in order to attach them.

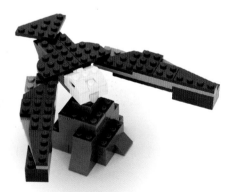

STEP 13: Design a base for your bird to perch on. The picture shows a 2 x 2 round tile with a hole at the top of the base, but the hole is not necessary for the design; any 2 x 2 tile will be just fine.

Now perch your bird on top of the base! If it doesn't balance, try adjusting the position of the wings. How cool is that?

POWERFUL PULLEYS

Here's another contraption that provides an amazing mechanical advantage for lifting. "Mechanical advantage" means that a machine increases the force that you put into it. In other words, it makes it easier for you to do a job. A pulley is simply a wheel with a groove, and it allows you to lift something up by pulling down. Multiply your lifting power by building a double-pulley system. You'll be amazed at how little force is required to lift a heavy load!

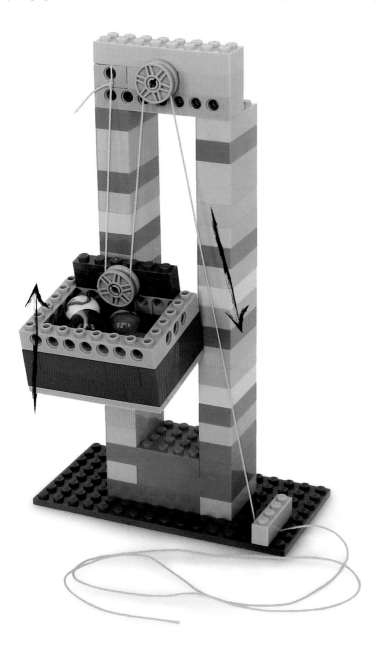

HOW IT WORKS

A one-pulley system, such as Professor Fiddlesticks' Wacky Tree House (page 168), does not actually increase the lifting power. However, using a simple pulley like this in real life makes lifting seem easier because pulling down is easier than lifting something up. You can get your weight into it!

To see some real mechanical power, you'll need a double-pulley system like the one in this project. In a double-pulley system, one wheel is attached to the load and the other is attached to a support structure. The amount of force needed to lift the load is reduced by half. When you pull the string down, you'll notice that you must pull it out twice as far as the load travels. Remember that all machines with mechanical advantage have a trade-off. Traveling a greater distance is the trade-off for using less effort or force, which is worth it when you're trying to lift something that otherwise would be too hard to lift.

Add another set of pulleys, and you'll multiply the force even more. With four pulleys, you'll need to pull out four times as much string as the distance the load moves. But as you can probably guess, you'll only need to use one-quarter as much force. That's some easy lifting!

PARTS LIST

DARK GRAY BRICKS
1—8 x 16 plate
1—1 x 6 plate
2—1 x 2 bricks
2—1 x 2 Technic bricks

LIGHT GRAY BRICKS
1—6 x 8 plate
1—1 x 8 Technic brick

3—1 x 2 Technic bricks
1—6 x 8 Technic brick, open center
4—Technic pins
4—wheels with a pin hole

RED BRICKS
4—1 x 6 bricks
3—1 x 4 bricks
3—1 x 2 bricks
2—1 x 3 bricks

BRICKS OF ANY COLOR
6—2 x 6 bricks
39—2 x 4 bricks
1—2 x 3 brick
2—1 x 2 bricks
1—2 x 8 brick

OTHER ITEMS
String
Marbles or coins

STEP 2: Build a basket to hold the weights. Start with a 6 x 8 plate and add two rows of bricks. A 6 x 8 Technic brick with an open center works well for the top of the basket because it's so strong.

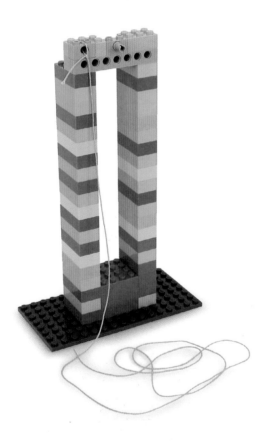

STEP 1: Construct a support frame for your pulleys that is 20 bricks high. You'll want it to be very sturdy so that the weight of the basket full of marbles won't pull it down. Place a 1 x 8 Technic brick across the top of the frame. Put a 1 x 2 Technic brick with a light gray pin in the center. Tie a string to a 1 x 2 Technic brick and place this on the top left corner. Add bricks to fill in between the Technic bricks.

STEP 3: Gather the bricks shown for attaching the pulley wheel.

STEP 4: Place two 1 x 2 bricks and a 1 x 2 Technic brick with a light gray pin on the back of the basket.

STEP 5: Attach the wheel and place a 1 x 6 plate on top to hold the wheel firmly in place. Fill the basket with marbles, or use coins as weights. Another good object to use as a weight is a handful of small stones.

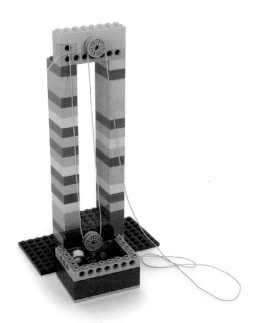

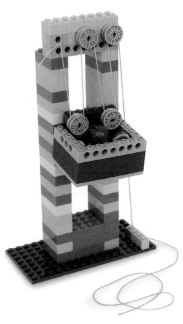

STEP 6: Attach a wheel to the pin at the top of the frame. Add a row of bricks across the top of the frame to hold the pulley wheel firmly in place. Then thread the string under the pulley on the basket and over the pulley on the frame. Now you're ready to test your double-pulley system! Pull the string down with your hand. If you want to keep the basket in place, attach a brick to the baseplate to secure the string.

Now try a system of four pulleys. Add a second pulley to the basket and a second pulley to the support frame. Thread your string through the pulleys and give it a pull. Wow, what do you notice about how much force is required? You'll also notice that with all that string threaded back and forth, you have to do a lot of pulling. That's okay, though, because the work was so easy!

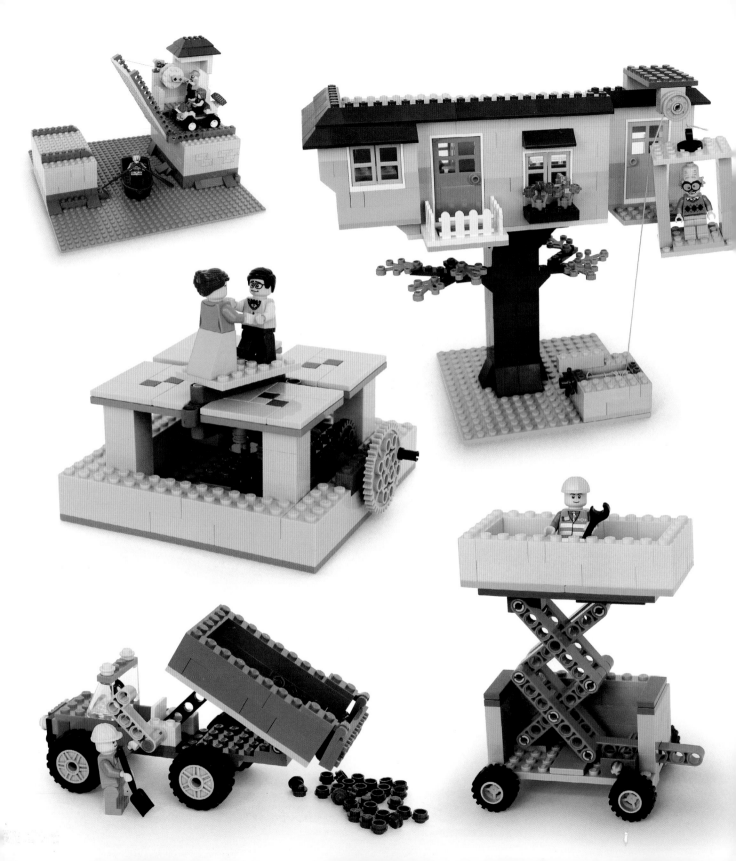

INVENT AND IMAGINE

Build clever inventions that double as imaginative scenes for your minifigure worlds! Create a merry-go-round that spins when you turn a handle. Build a motorized knight duel and a secret treasure cave with a hidden sliding door. Create a clever mechanism that will make your minifigures waltz across a ballroom dance floor. Then build a construction scene with several working machines, including a dump truck that really dumps its load. Building exciting worlds for your minifigures is even more fun when you add real inventions and clever moving parts!

CONSTRUCTION CRANE

This fully functional construction crane is loaded with awesome features. Turn a gear to raise and lower the load. The load will stay in place at any height thanks to a clever ratcheting system. Then use the handle on the side of the crane's base to turn the boom in either direction. Build the dump truck (page 132) and the scissor lift (page 136), and you'll have a complete construction site!

HOW IT WORKS

A worm gear and a 24-tooth gear inside the crane's base create the rotational motion of the boom. When you turn the handle, the axle turns the worm gear. The worm gear then turns the 24-tooth gear, which turns a vertical axle and moves the body of the crane.

Just like the Wind-Up Catapult (page 95), this crane uses a ratchet to keep the hook at the correct height. Without the ratchet, the string would unwind itself and the hook would sink to the ground any time you attach a heavy load. The pawl connects with the teeth in the gear on the crane's boom and keeps it from turning back the other way. You can raise your load, and it will stay that way! Simply lift the pawl to allow the hook to move downward again.

DID YOU KNOW?

Bridges, roads, subway systems and other major structures are designed by civil engineers. Within civil engineering there are several subdisciplines. For example, structural engineers design buildings and oversee construction projects while environmental engineers design the structures needed to deliver clean water to homes and businesses. If you love to build things, civil engineering may be the perfect career for you!

PARTS LIST

YELLOW BRICKS
2—4 x 6 plates
1—2 x 8 Technic plate (or regular plate)
1—2 x 4 plate
1—2 x 2 plate
2—1 x 4 plates
1—1 x 2 plate
1—1 x 6 tile
1—2 x 6 brick
2—1 x 6 bricks
3—1 x 4 bricks
1—1 x 2 brick
1—1 x 1 brick
2—1 x 9 liftarms

BLACK BRICKS
2—1 x 10 Technic bricks
2—1 x 8 Technic bricks
1—6 x 6 round plate

2—1 x 15 Technic liftarms
6—Technic pins with friction ridges lengthwise and center slots
1—Technic axle, 12 studs long
2—Technic axles, 10 studs long
1—steering wheel
64—link treads

DARK GRAY BRICKS
1—Technic connector #1
7—Technic gears, 24 tooth (only three are required if you substitute wheels for the tracks)
4—1 x 2 Technic bricks
1—Technic gear, 8 tooth
1—1 x 3 plate
1—2 x 2 round tile with a hole
1—2 x 2 brick with two pins
3—Technic axles, 4 studs long with a stop
1—hook with towball

LIGHT GRAY BRICKS
1—wedge belt wheel
4—1 x 4 Technic bricks
2—wheels with pin holes
1—1 x 2 Technic brick
5—Technic bushes
1—Technic bush, ½ length
1—Technic worm gear
1—Technic axle, 3 studs long
1—1 x 3 Technic liftarm with two axle holes and pin/crank
2—Technic pins

ASSORTED BRICKS
3—red Technic bushes
1—tan Technic axle pin without friction ridges
1—chair
2—levers (antennas)

OTHER ITEMS
String

STEP 1: Place a 1 x 8 black Technic brick on top of a 1 x 10 black Technic brick. Make two of these.

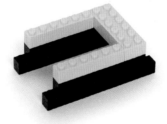

STEP 2: Connect the two sections with a 2 x 6 yellow brick. Add two 1 x 6 yellow bricks.

STEP 3: Slide an axle (12 studs long) through the second holes from the end on the top Technic bricks. Add two red Technic bushes and the worm gear. Then slide on a 1 x 3 light gray liftarm with two axle holes and a pin/crank.

STEP 4: Gather the bricks shown.

STEP 5: Attach the black 6 x 6 round plate and the 2 x 2 round tile with a hole to the top of the frame.

STEP 6: Slide a 24-tooth gear and a Technic bush onto an axle (4 studs long with a stop).

STEP 7: Insert the axle into the hole in the black 6 x 6 round plate so that it meshes with the worm gear. It won't actually be attached until step 24, but this is how it fits.

STEP 8: Place a 1 x 6 yellow tile on top of a 1 x 4 yellow brick.

STEP 9: Attach the yellow bricks to the end of the frame.

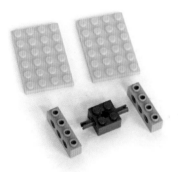

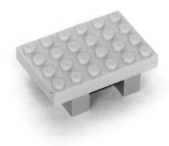

STEP 10: Find two 4 x 6 yellow plates, two 1 x 4 light gray Technic bricks and a 2 x 2 dark gray brick with two pins.

STEP 11: Attach the Technic bricks to the pins using the center hole on each. Stack the two 4 x 6 yellow plates.

STEP 12: Attach the yellow plates to the gray bricks.

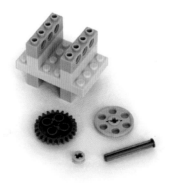

STEP 13: Add two 1 x 4 yellow bricks and two 1 x 4 light gray Technic bricks.

STEP 14: Find an axle (4 studs long with a stop), a 24-tooth gear, a wedge belt wheel and a Technic bush (½ length).

STEP 15: From right to left, slide the axle through the Technic brick, the Technic bush (½ length), the wedge belt wheel, the 24-tooth Technic gear and the other Technic brick.

STEP 16: Use an axle (3 studs long) to attach an 8-tooth Technic gear and a 24-tooth gear on the left side.

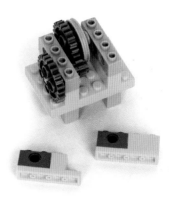

STEP 17: Grab two 1 x 4 yellow plates. Add a 1 x 2 dark gray Technic brick and a 1 x 1 yellow brick to one, and a 1 x 2 dark gray Technic brick and a 1 x 2 yellow brick to the other.

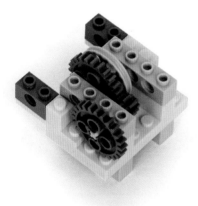

STEP 18: Attach the bricks from step 17 as shown.

STEP 19: Insert a black pin into each 1 x 2 dark gray Technic brick, on the inside. Attach a 1 x 15 black liftarm to each one. Tie a piece of string to a hole in the wedge belt wheel. Tie a hook to the other end. Wrap the excess string around the Technic bush (½ length). Then gather the bricks shown.

STEP 20: Use a gray pin to attach a wheel to the sixth hole on the black liftarm. Use an axle (4 studs long with a stop) to attach another wheel and a Technic bush to the top hole.

STEP 21: Add two more 1 x 2 dark gray Technic bricks and two black pins to the top of the mechanism.

STEP 22: Attach two 1 x 9 yellow liftarms to the black pins, and then use two more black pins to attach the other ends to the seventh hole from the top on the black liftarms. This will add stability to the design.

STEP 23: Get ready to attach the crane to the axle on the base. Note that the axle will not stick out of the base like this on its own. It's propped up so that you can see what you are supposed to attach.

STEP 24: Put your finger under the base and push up the gear and axle. Then attach the 2 x 2 dark gray brick on the bottom of the crane to the axle. You should be able to turn the 24-tooth gear on the left side to raise and lower the hook.

STEP 25: Now build a pawl to keep the string from unwinding when you attach a load to the hook. Gather the bricks shown.

STEP 26: Slide the gray pin into the Technic brick. Then attach the dark gray Technic connector #1. Insert the axle end of the tan pin into the connector.

STEP 27: Attach the pawl to the crane. It should connect with the 24-tooth gear that sits right next to the wedge belt wheel.

STEP 28: Find two axles (10 studs long), four Technic bushes and four 24-tooth gears.

STEP 29: Slide the axles through the last hole on each Technic brick. Add a Technic bush on each side, then a 24-tooth gear.

STEP 30: Attach the tracks to the gears. If you don't have tracks, substitute with wheels that have an X-shaped axle hole. You can also attach pins to the black Technic bricks and use wheels with pin holes.

STEP 31: Build a seat for the driver. Attach a 2 x 8 yellow Technic plate to the front of the crane under the black liftarms. A regular 2 x 8 plate will work just as well if you don't have the Technic plate. Then gather the bricks shown.

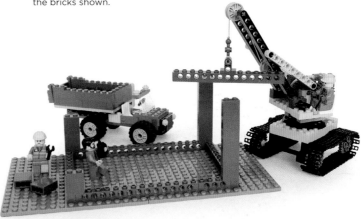

STEP 32: Attach the 2 x 2 plate to the 2 x 4 plate. Then add the chair and levers. Attach this to the 2 x 8 Technic plate so that it overlaps by one row of studs. Then find a construction worker to operate the crane!

Now put your crane to work! A Technic pin connector plate is very useful for allowing your crane to lift beams at a construction site. Use bricks to create the frame of a building that is in progress.

INVENT AND IMAGINE

HARDWORKING DUMP TRUCK

No construction site is complete without a dump truck! Construct a LEGO dump truck that is fully functional. The back gate swivels open, and you can turn a lever to raise the bed of the truck and dump its load.

HOW IT WORKS

The mechanism on this dump truck is simple yet smart. Use a lever to apply force at one location to create motion at another location. Build a lever with a handle that forms a 90-degree angle. When you rotate the handle down, the lever will exert an upward force on the bed of the dump truck. Open the tailgate before lifting the bed, and out dumps the load! The bed of the dump truck is lined with tiles to reduce friction so that the load will dump more quickly and completely.

PARTS LIST

DARK GRAY BRICKS
2—1 x 6 bricks
6—1 x 4 bricks
3—1 x 3 bricks
1—1 x 2 brick
1—1 x 2 brick
2—1 x 1 bricks with a stud on the side (headlight)
2—1 x 2 plates with a pin hole on top
1—2 x 6 plate
1—1 x 2 plate
1—4 x 12 plate
1—4 x 6 plate
2—1 x 2 plates with a clip on the end
2—1 x 2 plates with a handle on the end

2—1 x 2 grills
1—Technic axle, 4 studs long with a stop

LIGHT GRAY BRICKS
1—6 x 10 plate
4—2 x 4 tiles
2—2 x 4 plates with two pins
1—2 x 2 plate with pin hole
1—2 x 4 Technic liftarm, L-shape, thick
1—Technic bush
2—Technic pins

BLUE BRICKS
1—2 x 4 brick
1—1 x 2 brick
2—1 x 4 plates
1—2 x 4 plate

2—1 x 2 plates
2—car doors

ASSORTED BRICKS
1—2 x 4 black plate
1—1 x 5 black Technic liftarm, thin
1—1 x 2 yellow brick
1—1 x 2 yellow Technic brick
4—1 x 1 yellow round plates
1—2 x 4 windshield
4—wheels
1—white chair
1—steering wheel

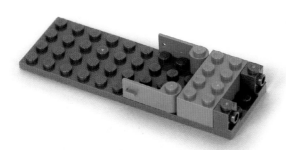

STEP 1: Grab a 4 x 12 dark gray plate. Attach two 1 x 1 dark gray bricks with a stud on the side (headlight), a blue 2 x 4 brick and two car doors.

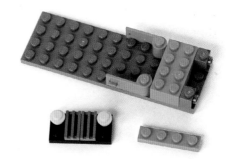

STEP 2: Build the front grill. Attach two 1 x 2 grills and two 1 x 1 yellow round plates to a 2 x 4 black plate.

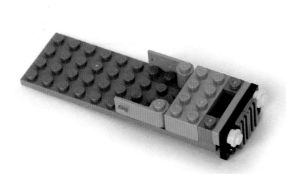

STEP 3: Place a 1 x 4 blue plate on the front of the truck. Then add the 2 x 4 black plate.

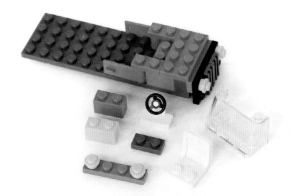

STEP 4: Add a 2 x 4 blue plate and two 1 x 2 blue plates to the truck. Then gather the bricks shown. Attach two 1 x 1 yellow round plates to a 1 x 4 blue plate.

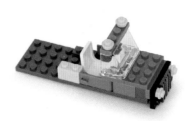

STEP 5: Place the steering wheel on top of a 1 x 2 blue brick and attach both to the truck. Then add the chair. Place a 1 x 2 dark gray plate on the left side of the truck and a 1 x 2 yellow brick on the right side.

STEP 6: Attach the windshield and place the 1 x 4 blue plate on top of it.

STEP 7: Add a 4 x 6 plate to the back of the truck so that it overlaps by three rows of studs. Gather the bricks shown for building the mechanism.

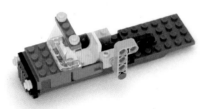

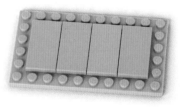

STEP 8: Slide the liftarms, Technic bush and 1 x 2 Technic brick onto the axle in the order shown.

STEP 9: Attach the mechanism to the 1 x 2 dark gray plate on the side of the truck. Rotate the axle so that the black liftarm is down and the light gray liftarm is up before attaching it.

STEP 10: Build the dump truck's bed. Attach four 2 x 4 tiles to a 6 x 10 plate.

STEP 11: Add two layers of dark gray bricks around three sides of the bed.

STEP 12: Build a tailgate that can raise and lower. Attach two 1 x 2 plates with clips on the ends to the back of the truck's bed. Then find a 2 x 6 plate and two 1 x 2 plates with a handle on the end.

STEP 13: Attach the 1 x 2 plates with handles to the 2 x 6 plate. Then attach this to the clips.

STEP 14: Find two light gray pins, a 2 x 2 plate with a pin hole on the bottom and two 1 x 2 plates with a pin hole on the top.

STEP 15: Use the pins to connect the plates as shown. Then turn the truck bed upside down.

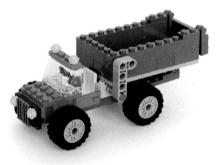

STEP 16: Attach the 2 x 2 plate to the underside of the dump truck's bed.

STEP 17: Add two 2 x 4 plates with two pins to the bottom of the truck and attach the wheels.

STEP 18: Use the two 1 x 2 dark gray plates with a pin hole on top to attach the bed to the truck, and the dump truck is complete!

Test out the mechanism to make sure it's working correctly. Push the handle down, and the truck bed will lift.

Then find a construction figure to drive the truck! Brown 1 x 1 round plates look great as dirt, but really you can fill your truck with any color and size of bricks. What type of work will your dump truck do first?

SCISSOR LIFT

Have you ever seen a scissor lift at work? They are very useful for construction and maintenance work both indoors and outdoors. A scissor lift is built from pairs of crisscrossing supports that open and close just like scissors. This scissor lift will boost up your minifigures so that they can install windows at a construction site or repair the ceiling on a tall building.

HOW IT WORKS

A scissor lift is basically a series of levers used to transfer motion from a horizontal direction to a vertical direction. Real industrial scissor lifts use hydraulics, or fluid-filled cylinders, to create the motion. As the cylinders fill with fluid, they push the scissor legs closer together, which raises the platform. This LEGO scissor lift doesn't have hydraulics of course, but the principle is the same. Push on the liftarm that is sticking out of the side of the machine. It will push the scissor legs closer together and raise the platform.

PARTS LIST

LIGHT GRAY BRICKS
1—6 x 10 plate
2—6 x 6 plates
1—1 x 8 plate
1—1 x 2 plate
3—1 x 6 bricks
4—1 x 4 bricks
4—1 x 3 bricks
3—1 x 2 bricks
1—1 x 1 brick
1—2 x 4 tile

4—2 x 2 plates with a wheel holder
1—Technic axle, 5 studs long
4—Technic pins, 3 studs long
7—Technic pins

DARK GRAY BRICKS
3—1 x 2 Technic bricks
2—1 x 4 plates
2—2 x 4 plates
1—4 x 10 plate
2—1 x 4 tiles
4—wheels

BLUE BRICKS
9—1 x 7 Technic liftarms
1—2 x 2 plate

YELLOW BRICKS
6—1 x 6 bricks
5—1 x 3 bricks
6—1 x 2 bricks
1—1 x 1 brick

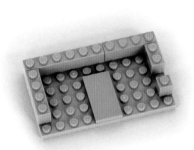

STEP 1: Begin making the base of the scissor lift by attaching bricks and a 2 x 4 tile to a 6 x 10 plate as shown.

STEP 2: Gather the bricks shown.

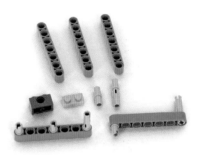

STEP 3: Grab two 1 x 7 Technic liftarms and insert light gray pins into the holes as shown. For this project, some of the pins will need to be 3 studs long.

STEP 4: Place the right liftarm on top of the left. Attach a 1 x 2 plate to a 1 x 2 Technic brick and slide it onto the pin (3 studs long) on the bottom left. Attach another 1 x 7 liftarm to the pin (3 studs long) on the bottom right.

STEP 5: Build a second "X" with the remaining two liftarms.

STEP 6: Gather the bricks shown for building the second layer of liftarms.

STEP 7: Attach a liftarm to the pin (3 studs long) sticking out of the Technic brick. Insert two more light gray pins into that liftarm. Gather a 1 x 2 dark gray Technic brick and a 2 x 2 blue plate.

STEP 8: Place a 2 x 2 blue plate on top of a 1 x 2 dark gray Technic brick. Slide this onto the pin at the top left of the scissor lift. Grab another 1 x 7 liftarm and insert a pin on one end.

STEP 9: Turn the liftarm with a pin so that the pin is facing up and attach it to the top right pin on the scissor lift.

STEP 10: Attach the final two pins. Test your mechanism to make sure that it will fold and unfold correctly.

STEP 11: Attach the scissor mechanism to the base from step 1. Add two more layers of gray bricks, but leave a hole for the liftarm to stick out on the side.

STEP 12: Add a 1 x 8 light gray plate on the back of the frame. Then place a 1 x 4 dark gray plate and a 1 x 4 dark gray tile on each side.

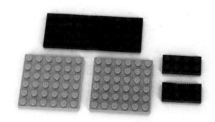

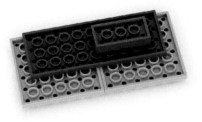

STEP 13: Build the platform for the worker to stand on. Grab the plates shown.

STEP 14: Use the 4 x 10 dark gray plate to connect the two 6 x 6 light gray plates. Stack two 2 x 4 plates and attach them underneath as shown.

STEP 15: Build two rows of yellow bricks on top of the platform.

STEP 16: Attach the platform to the 2 x 2 blue plate on top of the scissor lift. The other side of the platform will just rest on the blue liftarms. If it were connected on both sides, it would not be able to raise and lower! Place a 1 x 2 dark gray Technic brick on the right corner of the base.

Raise your scissor lift by pushing on the blue liftarm, and keep it elevated by sliding an axle through the 1 x 2 Technic brick and then through the blue liftarm. Remove the axle to adjust the height of the scissor lift again.

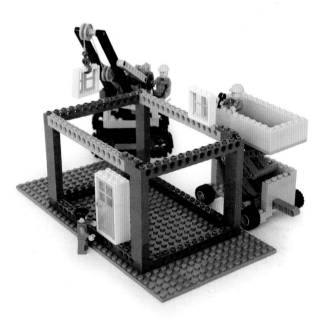

Elevate the scissor lift just a little, or raise it all the way! It can easily be adjusted for any type of construction job.

Create your own construction site! Use two 16 x 16 plates as a base. Use long Technic bricks to make a building frame, and use your crane (page 126) and your scissor lift to help the workers install the beams, windows and doors.

POWERFUL ROCK HAULER

Clear away rocks from a construction site with this fun little rock hauler. Using the lever on the back of the machine, you can lift a load, swivel the arm to the place you want it and then dump the load. Create a construction scene with the dump truck (page 132) or pair it with the crane (page 126) to lift heavy debris away from a work site.

HOW IT WORKS

This machine combines two types of motion. The arm of the rock hauler is a first-class lever. This means that the fulcrum, or pivot point of the lever, is located between the load and the effort. You push down on the handle, and the lever pivots and lifts the load. The location of the fulcrum is important if you want to increase the force of the machine. If you place the fulcrum close to the handle, you'll notice that it's very difficult to push the handle down. Move the fulcrum farther away from the point where you apply the effort, and you'll notice a huge difference. Your hand will have to travel farther, but you'll notice that lifting is now much easier! This is the trade-off for the mechanical advantage you now have.

You can control the dumping action of the bucket by building a four-bar linkage. Four rods are connected at four pivot points, which allows the handle at one end to control the motion at the other end.

DID YOU KNOW?

This rock hauler is a first-class lever. Other examples of first-class levers are a balance, a seesaw, a catapult and a furniture dolly. A pair of scissors is two first-class levers put together. Levers are super useful!

PARTS LIST

DARK GRAY BRICKS
4—1 x 15 Technic liftarms
1—1 x 9 Technic liftarm
2—1 x 4 Technic bricks
1—4 x 4 round brick
1—2 x 6 plate
1—1 x 2 brick with a pin on the side
1—1 x 2 brick
1—4 x 6 plate

LIGHT GRAY BRICKS
1—8 x 8 plate
4—2 x 4 tiles
2—1 x 2 tiles
2—1 x 2 plates

YELLOW BRICKS
4—1 x 6 bricks
4—1 x 4 bricks
4—1 x 2 bricks
2—1 x 1 slopes
1—2 x 2 brick
2—1 x 2 Technic bricks
1—1 x 2 Technic brick with an axle hole
1—1 x 4 plate
1—1 x 4 tile
1—1 x 1 plate with a vertical clip
1—1 x 1 plate

ASSORTED BRICKS
6—blue Technic pins with friction
ridges, 3 studs long

1—3 x 5 black L-shaped Technic
liftarm, thick
1—4 x 4 black turntable base, locking
2—white levers (antenna)
1—white chair
1—2 x 4 windshield

OTHER ITEMS
For a load to haul, use rocks, pebbles,
dry beans or small LEGO bricks.

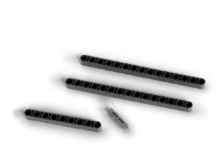

STEP 1: Grab two 1 x 15 liftarms, a 1 x 9 liftarm and a blue pin with friction ridges (3 studs long).

STEP 2: Use the blue pin to connect the liftarms. Place the 1 x 9 liftarm in the center, perpendicular to the others. Then grab another blue pin and a 3 x 5 black L-shaped liftarm.

STEP 3: Connect the black liftarm at the front using the blue pin. Then grab two more 1 x 15 liftarms and two more blue pins.

STEP 4: Insert the blue pins as shown.

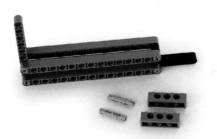

STEP 5: Attach the 1 x 15 liftarms as shown. Grab two 1 x 4 Technic bricks and two more blue pins. Technic bricks with studs will work nicely to create a way to attach the bucket.

STEP 6: Use the pins to attach the two 1 x 4 Technic bricks to the black L-shaped liftarm.

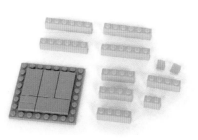

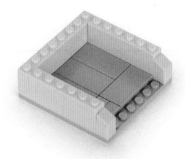

STEP 7: You now have a four-bar linkage. Test it to make sure it works. When you tilt the handle, the black L-shaped liftarm will tilt too.

STEP 8: Build the bucket. Start by attaching four 2 x 4 light gray tiles and two 1 x 2 light gray tiles to an 8 x 8 plate. Gather the yellow bricks shown.

STEP 9: Use yellow bricks to build a wall around three of the sides. Attach the two 1 x 1 slopes as shown.

STEP 10: Now build a swiveling base for your rock hauler. Gather the bricks shown.

STEP 11: Attach a 4 x 4 round brick to a 4 x 4 square turntable base. Then add a 2 x 6 plate.

STEP 12: Add a 1 x 2 yellow brick on one side and a 2 x 2 yellow brick on the other side. Then add a 1 x 2 dark gray brick and two 1 x 2 dark gray bricks with pins, one on each side. These will attach the base to the lever mechanism.

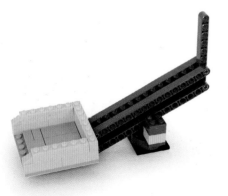

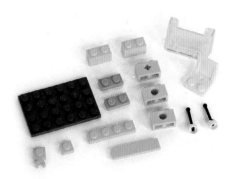

STEP 13: Attach the base to the lever mechanism. You'll need to remove the 1 x 2 gray bricks with a pin and attach them to the liftarms. Then reconnect them to the base.

STEP 14: Now build the cab. Gather the bricks shown.

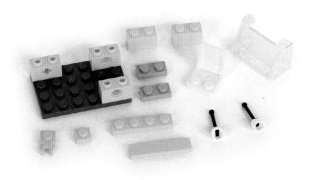

STEP 15: Attach two 1 x 2 Technic bricks and a 1 x 2 Technic brick with an X-shaped axle hole.

STEP 16: Add two 1 x 2 bricks to the front of the cab. Attach the chair. Stack the two 1 x 2 light gray plates and place them just in front of the chair.

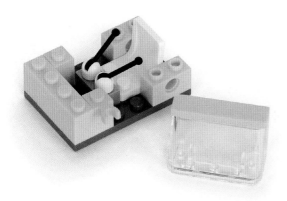

STEP 17: Add a 1 x 4 plate, a 1 x 1 plate and a 1 x 1 plate with a clip to the front of the cab. Place the two levers on top of the 1 x 2 light gray plates. Then put the 1 x 4 tile on top of the windshield.

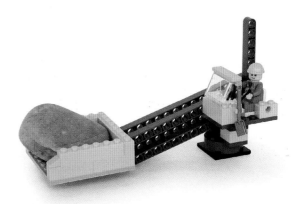

STEP 18: Attach the windshield to the cab. Then attach the cab to the base of the rock hauler. Your machine is now complete!

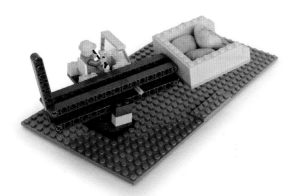

If you want to keep the arm in an elevated position, slide an axle between the levers and insert it into the 1 x 2 Technic brick with an X-shaped axle hole on the cab.

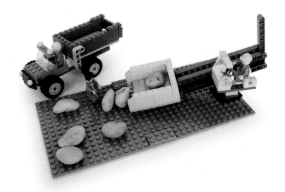

Now you're ready to assemble a construction scene! Pretend that construction workers are loading rocks and boulders into the rock hauler. Then use the lever to operate the arm and dump the rocks into the dump truck. When they finish, the truck can carry away the load and the workers will be ready to construct a building on level ground.

MINIFIGURE MERRY-GO-ROUND

Build a merry-go-round with horses that is just the right size for your minifigures! Turn the handle and the merry-go-round spins at just the right speed. After completing the merry-go-round, you just might want to invent an entire amusement park to go with it!

HOW IT WORKS

To make a working LEGO merry-go-round, you'll need to convert the motion generated by turning a vertical handle to a horizontal spinning platform. This can be accomplished with two gears whose teeth connect at a 90-degree angle. Spur gears aren't the best for this type of motion, but thankfully bevel gears are perfect! Instead of being flat, bevel gears have teeth that are curved at the edges to allow two gears to mesh together at an angle.

Real merry-go-rounds of the past used steam engines, but modern merry-go-rounds operate with electric motors that turn large belts. A wooden platform filled with wooden animals (and riders!) is a lot of weight to move, and the components must be extremely strong. Merry-go-rounds can also be works of art, however, with beautifully carved and painted horses or even a whole menagerie of animals.

PARTS LIST

LIME GREEN BRICKS
1—1 x 2 brick
2—1 x 4 bricks
2—1 x 6 bricks
1—2 x 4 brick
2—2 x 6 plates
1—1 x 6 plate

DARK GRAY BRICKS
1—2 x 4 Technic plate
2—2 x 2 round tiles with a hole
1—1 x 6 Technic brick
1—1 x 6 brick

1—1 x 6 plate
1—Technic gear, 8 tooth
1—Technic gear, 24 tooth

LIGHT GRAY BRICKS
1—1 x 6 brick
2—1 x 2 plates
1—1 x 6 Technic brick
1—2 x 6 Technic plate
1—Technic bevel gear, 20 tooth
1—Technic bevel gear, 12 tooth
2—Technic axles, 7 studs long
1—1 x 3 Technic liftarm with two axle
holes and a pin/crank

ASSORTED BRICKS
1—16 x 16 bright green plate
4—2 x 4 dark azure bricks
8—2 x 2 dark azure slopes, two bricks
high
4—2 x 4 medium azure plates
1—2 x 3 medium azure plate
1—6 x 6 medium azure round plate
1—black Technic axle, 12 studs long
4—red Technic bushes
1—1 x 6 Technic brick
2—2 x 2 yellow round plates
1—10 x 10 dark tan octagonal plate
4—horses
Flowers

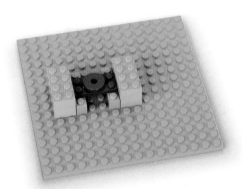

STEP 1: Grab a 16 x 16 plate. Begin the base of the merry-go-round with four 2 x 4 dark azure bricks, two 1 x 4 lime green bricks, a 2 x 4 dark gray Technic plate and a 2 x 2 dark gray tile with a hole.

STEP 2: Add four 2 x 2 dark azure slopes (two bricks high) on each side.

STEP 3: Place two 1 x 6 lime green bricks and a 2 x 4 lime green brick on the base. Then find the bricks shown.

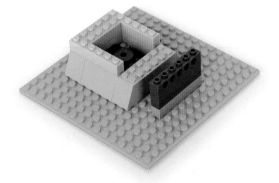

STEP 4: Stack the gray bricks as shown to create a place to hold the gears.

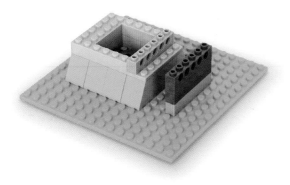

STEP 5: Add a 2 x 6 lime green plate and a 1 x 6 light gray Technic brick to the base.

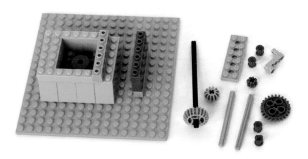

STEP 6: Slide a 20-tooth bevel gear onto an axle (12 studs long). Then gather the other bricks shown.

STEP 7: Insert the black axle into the hole in the 2 x 2 round tile at the center of the base. Slide an axle (7 studs long) through both Technic bricks and add two red Technic bushes, an 8-tooth gear and a 12-tooth bevel gear. Adjust the axle so that the two bevel gears connect.

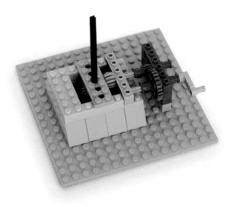

STEP 8: Slide the 2 x 6 light gray Technic plate over the black axle and attach it to the lime green bricks. It will keep the axle steady. Then add the other axle, Technic bush, 24-tooth gear and handle as shown.

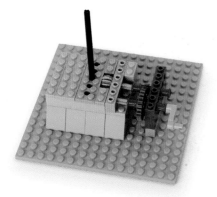

STEP 9: Add a 1 x 6 lime green plate, a 2 x 6 lime green plate, two 1 x 2 light gray plates and a 1 x 2 lime green brick to the base.

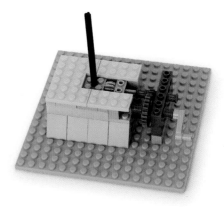

STEP 10: Cover the mechanism with four 2 x 4 medium azure plates and a 2 x 3 medium azure plate.

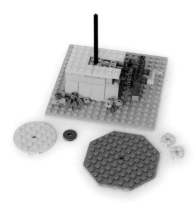

STEP 11: Gather the bricks shown to build the platform for the merry-go-round.

STEP 12: Slide the 6 x 6 round plate and the 2 x 2 round tile over the black axle and attach them to the base. Attach a 2 x 2 yellow round plate to both sides of the 10 x 10 octagonal plate.

STEP 13: Slide the platform onto the black axle and load it up with horses. Then find some minifigures to take on a ride. Turn the handle and watch your merry-go-round spin!

Create a fun amusement park scene by adding a ticket booth and a park bench to your merry-go-round! Then see if you can design more rides and games for your minifigures to enjoy.

To create the ticket booth, build a three-sided structure on a 6 x 8 plate. Leave an opening for the ticket window, and use a 2 x 4 tile to create a counter. Add 2 x 3 slope bricks for roof tiles or substitute a different type of slope. You can build a simple bench by putting a 2 x 8 plate and two 1 x 8 bricks on top of two 1 x 3 bricks.

BALLROOM DANCE FLOOR

Build a whimsical scene with minifigures that turn and move around a dance floor. This project is reminiscent of classic music boxes that feature a ballerina who dances when you open the lid. Turn the handle and watch your minifigures waltz in a pattern around the dance floor. You can also animate this project with a motor and battery box so that the minifigures can dance on their own.

HOW IT WORKS

The mechanism in the dance floor is based on an ancient machine called the Trammel of Archimedes. It's a fascinating device that was used in the past to draw perfect ellipses. The dance floor mechanism has two shuttles that run back and forth in channels that are perpendicular to each other. The shuttles are powered by an arm underneath them that spins in a circle. The circular motion of the arm is converted to the back-and-forth motion of the shuttles. A LEGO plate attached to both shuttles follows an interesting path as the machine turns and creates a lovely dance pattern.

As you turn the handle and the minifigures dance, pay attention to the motion of each individual dancer. The dancers turn and spin because they are mounted to a plate attached to the shuttles. They each follow the path of one of the shuttles. It's quite enjoyable to watch!

PARTS LIST

TAN BRICKS
13—2 x 6 bricks
5—2 x 4 bricks
2—2 x 3 bricks
20—2 x 2 bricks
2—1 x 3 bricks
2—1 x 2 bricks
1—4 x 6 plate
2—2 x 6 plates
16—2 x 4 tiles
8—1 x 1 tiles
2—Technic pins, 3 studs long
1—Technic axle pin

LIGHT GRAY BRICKS
1—2 x 8 Technic plate
1—1 x 8 plate
4—2 x 2 plates
1—1 x 6 brick
2—1 x 2 bricks
2—Technic axles, 5 studs long
1—Technic axle, 3 studs long
1—1 x 4 Technic liftarm with two
   axle holes, thin
2—Technic bushes, ½ length
1— Technic gear, 40 tooth
2—Technic bevel gears, 12 tooth

DARK GRAY BRICKS
1—2 x 8 Technic plate
2—1 x 6 plates
2—1 x 4 plates
1—1 x 6 Technic brick
2—1 x 7 Technic liftarms
2—1 x 3 Technic liftarms
1—2 x 2 round tile with a hole
1—Technic gear, 24 tooth
1—Technic gear, 8 tooth
1—Technic axle, 4 studs long with
   a stop

ASSORTED BRICKS
1—16 x 16 dark tan plate
1—1 x 6 red Technic brick
2—red Technic bushes
1—1 x 8 black Technic brick
2—black Technic bevel gears, 20
   tooth
2—blue Technic pins, ½ length
4—6 x 6 blue plates
8—1 x 1 red tiles
1—black Technic pin with friction
   ridges
Motor and battery box (optional)

DID YOU KNOW?

Archimedes was a famous scientist, mathematician and inventor born in approximately 287 BC. His accomplishments and discoveries are numerous, but among his most well known are his calculations of the value of pi, his discovery of a formula for calculating the area and surface area of a sphere, his invention of a screw that can be used to lift water and his work with levers and pulleys. Archimedes is known for saying, "Give me a lever long enough and a fulcrum on which to place it, and I shall move the world."

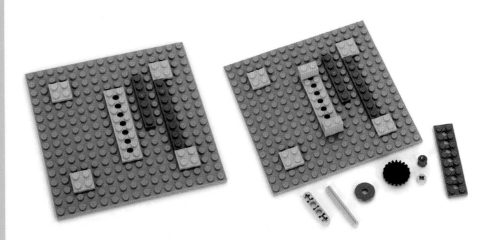

STEP 1: Grab a 16 x 16 plate. Attach the plates to it as shown.

STEP 2: Place a 1 x 2 light gray brick on each end of the 2 x 8 light gray Technic plate. Then gather the bricks shown. The gear is a 20-tooth Technic bevel gear.

STEP 3: Attach the 2 x 2 round tile with a hole in the center to a 2 x 8 Technic plate. Then insert an axle (5 studs long) and slide on a red Technic bush underneath the plate.

STEP 4: Attach the 2 x 8 dark gray Technic plate to the two 1 x 2 light gray bricks. Slide a Technic bush (½ length) and a 1 x 4 thin liftarm onto the top of the axle.

STEP 5: Add a 1 x 6 dark gray plate and a 1 x 8 light gray plate to the base. Then find the bricks shown.

STEP 6: Place two 1 x 3 tan bricks and a 1 x 8 black Technic brick on top of the light gray plate. Place a 1 x 6 light gray brick and a 1 x 6 dark gray Technic brick on top of the two dark gray plates.

STEP 7: Slide an axle (3 studs long) through the first hole in the 1 x 6 dark gray Technic brick and add a 12-tooth Technic bevel gear and a 20-tooth Technic bevel gear. You may want to remove the bricks to add the gears and then reattach them.

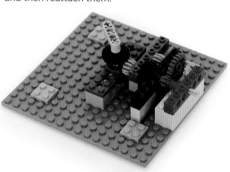

STEP 8: Add the axle (4 studs long) and the 24-tooth Technic gear and the 12-tooth Technic bevel gear. The stop on the axle should be on the inside edge of the dark gray Technic brick.

STEP 9: Place one 2 x 6 tan brick and two 2 x 6 tan plates next to the gears. Add a 1 x 6 red Technic brick.

STEP 10: Slide the axle through the red Technic brick and add a Technic bush and an 8-tooth gear. The axle should go into the black Technic brick as well. When you turn the light gray axle, all the gears should move smoothly. Adjust the gears and axles if needed.

STEP 11: Grab two 1 x 7 liftarms and two 1 x 3 liftarms. Then find the pins shown.

STEP 12: Insert two pins (3 studs long) into the end holes on a 1 x 7 liftarm, and then add the two 1 x 3 liftarms.

STEP 13: Attach the second 1 x 7 liftarm and insert the two blue pins (½ length).

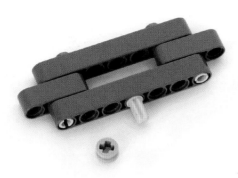

STEP 14: Insert the tan axle pin into the center hole of the bottom liftarm.

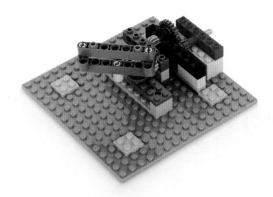

STEP 15: Slide the liftarm assembly into the axle hole on the light gray thin liftarm. Attach the Technic bush (½ length) underneath the thin liftarm to hold the tan axle pin in place.

STEP 16: Build two layers of tan bricks around the perimeter of the base.

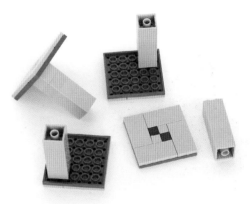

STEP 17: Use four 6 x 6 blue plates to build the dance floor surface. Decorate each with tiles as shown, or create your own pattern for the dance floor. Then build a base of five 2 x 2 bricks for each section. Attach the 2 x 2 columns exactly as shown—spacing is very important.

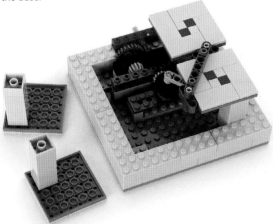

STEP 18: Attach the floor sections to the base one at a time. Each one should sit on top of a 2 x 2 light gray plate. As you add them, direct the shuttles into their channels between the floor sections.

STEP 19: The completed floor should look like this.

STEP 20: Attach a 40-tooth gear and a black pin. The black pin is a handle for turning the mechanism. Then attach a 4 x 6 plate for the dancers to ride on.

STEP 21: Now grab some minifigures to be dancers! You can create a skirt by using a 2 x 2 slope (two bricks high).

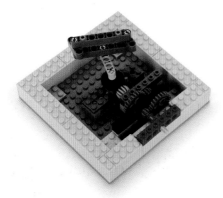

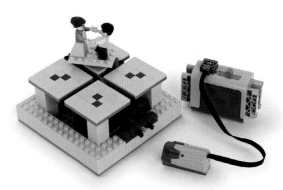

STEP 22: To motorize the dance floor, swap out the 12-tooth bevel gear and 20-tooth bevel gear with a 24-tooth gear and an 8-tooth gear. The speed of the motor is very fast, so you'll need to gear it down a little bit.

STEP 23: Add two black pins and attach the motor to the light gray axle and both black pins.

STEP 24: Turn it on and watch your minifigures dance!

BUILDING TIP

If the machine seems to "catch" a little either in manual mode or with the motor, check to make sure that none of the parts are rubbing on each other. The axle that is in the thin liftarm (step 4) could be a culprit. Make sure that the axle is not sticking out at all, or it will catch on the dark gray liftarm as it turns. Also, check to be sure that each section of the floor is attached tightly.

COASTAL DRAWBRIDGE

Sometimes bridges must be constructed over water for cars to drive on, but they are too low for large boats to safely pass under. The solution to a busy waterway is to make the bridge a drawbridge! When a boat comes along, the bridge can be raised and the boat can travel through. Once the boat has had its turn, the bridge is lowered again and the cars can go back to driving on the bridge. What a great solution! Construct a LEGO drawbridge and pretend that cars and boats are taking turns traveling around the coast.

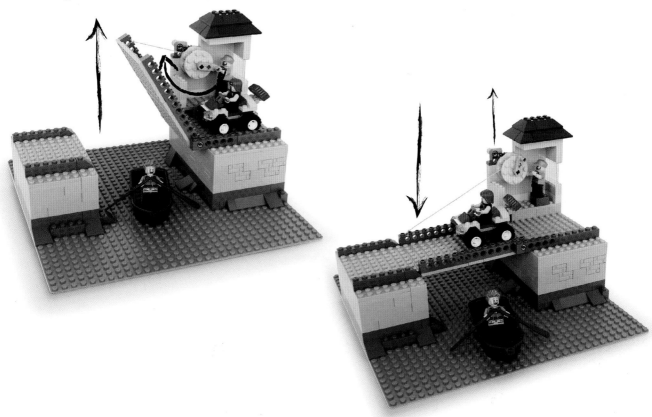

HOW IT WORKS

Raise your LEGO drawbridge by turning the winch and winding up the string. The string pulls the edge of the bridge upward. Use a ratchet mechanism to keep the string from unwinding from the weight of the bridge. Lift the pawl to release the gear when you are ready to put the bridge down again.

This LEGO drawbridge doesn't have much weight to be concerned about, but both ancient and modern drawbridges use counterweights to help balance the weight of the bridge and to make it easier to lift. Modern drawbridges use an electric or oil-powered motor to do the lifting, and many of them lift up in two sections with an opening for boats in the middle.

PARTS LIST

BASE
1—32 x 32 blue baseplate
Various light gray bricks for building the bases
Various dark gray bricks and slopes for building the bases
4—4 x 10 light gray plates
1—8 x 8 light gray plate
1—6 x 6 light gray plate
1—2 x 6 light gray plate

BRIDGE AND MECHANISM

LIGHT GRAY BRICKS
3—2 x 4 bricks
1—2 x 3 brick
1—4 x 10 plate
1—8 x 8 plate
2—6 x 10 plates

1—2 x 10 plate
1—1 x 6 Technic brick
1—Technic connector #1
1—1 x 3 Technic liftarm with two axle holes and a pin/crank
3—Technic pins

DARK GRAY BRICKS
1—Technic gear, 24-tooth
2—1 x 14 Technic bricks
1—1 x 6 Technic brick
3—1 x 6 bricks
2—1 x 2 slopes
1—2 x 2 brick
1—Technic pin connector plate with two holes

TAN BRICKS
9—1 x 4 bricks
4—1 x 3 bricks

5—1 x 2 bricks
2—1 x 1 bricks
2—2 x 6 bricks
1—1 x 4 Technic brick

ASSORTED BRICKS
2—1 x 4 dark blue slopes
8—2 x 2 dark blue corner slopes
4—2 x 2 dark blue slopes
1—1 x 4 x 3 clear panel
4—1 x 4 light azure bricks
1—black Technic axle, 6 studs long
2—4 x 4 yellow round plates
1—2 x 2 red round brick

OTHER ITEMS
String

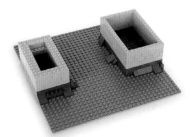

STEP 1: Build two bases for either side of the bridge. The base on the left is 8 studs by 14 studs on the outside row. The base on the right is 10 studs by 16 studs. It's fine to use either bricks that are 1 stud wide or 2 studs wide. Make your scene look like a rocky coast by putting some dark gray slope bricks at the water's edge.

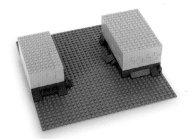

STEP 2: Cover the bases with plates. The base on the left has an 8 x 8 plate, a 6 x 6 plate and a 2 x 6 plate. The base on the right has four 4 x 10 plates.

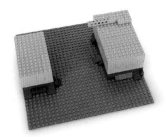

STEP 3: Place a 1 x 6 Technic brick, three 2 x 4 bricks and a 2 x 3 brick on the base on the right.

STEP 4: Cover the bricks you added in step 3 with a 4 x 10 plate. Then add four 1 x 4 light azure bricks, or substitute another color.

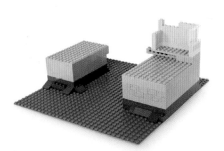

STEP 5: Use tan bricks to build the gatekeeper's building as shown.

STEP 6: Gather the bricks and materials shown for building the winch.

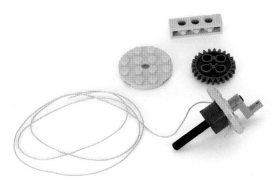

STEP 7: Slide the 1 x 3 liftarm with two axle holes and a pin, a 4 x 4 yellow round plate and a 2 x 2 red round brick onto the axle. If you tie the string around the red round brick, it won't have enough friction to keep it from just spinning when you turn the handle. Place the string between the yellow and red bricks, and then attach them to each other to secure the string.

STEP 8: Attach the second 4 x 4 yellow plate. Then slide the 1 x 4 Technic brick onto the axle and then finally the 24-tooth gear.

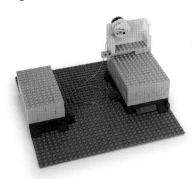

STEP 9: Place the winch on the gatekeeper's building as shown.

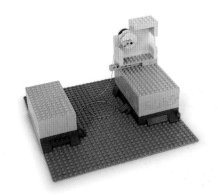

STEP 10: Add two more layers of tan bricks to the right side of the gatekeeper's building. Then place two 2 x 6 tan bricks on top.

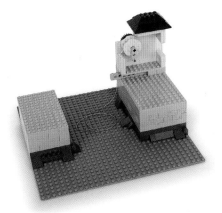

STEP 11: Build a little roof on the gatekeeper's building with dark blue slope bricks.

STEP 12: Assemble the bridge. Use two 1 x 14 Technic bricks to connect two 6 x 10 plates and a 2 x 10 plate. Insert two gray pins in the end as shown.

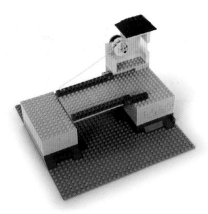

STEP 13: Add a 1 x 6 dark gray Technic brick to the base, and then connect the bridge to the base on both sides using the gray pins. Tie the end of the string to the last hole on the 1 x 14 Technic brick.

STEP 14: Find a Technic pin connector plate with two holes, a light gray pin and a Technic pin connector #1.

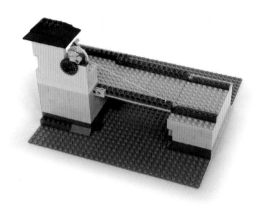

STEP 15: Attach them as shown to build the pawl for the bridge.

STEP 16: Place the pawl on the gatekeeper's building so that it connects with the teeth of the 24-tooth gear.

STEP 17: Add a 2 x 2 brick for the gatekeeper to stand on and gray bricks to mark the boundaries of the road. Place an 8 x 8 light gray plate on the left side base to make it just the right height for cars to travel across. Your bridge is now complete!

Find a vehicle for the road and tell the driver to wait while a boat crosses under the bridge. Turn the crank to raise the bridge and watch how the pawl keeps it in position. If you want to expand your road, add 32 x 32 baseplates on either side and build roads that connect.

MEDIEVAL KNIGHT DUEL

Create a motorized knight battle! Turn on the motor, and your knights will duel, sliding back and forth while brandishing their swords. See which knight can last the longest without falling off his platform!

HOW IT WORKS

This clever contraption uses a crank to convert circular motion to lateral motion. The crank is made up of the wheel (a 40-tooth gear and a 1 x 2 liftarm), a rod (axle) and a platform that slides back and forth. The axle is attached to the wheel with a gray pin, which allows it to rotate freely. The platform is also attached to the axle with a gray pin, so it moves freely as well. When you turn on the motor and the gears spin, the rod moves in an off-center circle and pushes the platform back and forth. Isn't that cool? This type of mechanism works great for making two knights duel each other. Can you think of any other uses for this type of motion?

PARTS LIST

DARK GRAY BRICKS
3—Technic gears, 24 tooth
1—Technic gear, 8 tooth
1—1 x 14 Technic brick
4—1 x 2 Technic bricks
2—1 x 2 bricks
2—2 x 2 bricks
4—Technic connectors #1

LIGHT GRAY BRICKS
2—Technic gears, 40 tooth
2—1 x 8 Technic bricks
4—2 x 4 tiles

2—1 x 6 tiles
1—1 x 4 tile
2—2 x 2 plates
2—1 x 2 Technic liftarms with a pin
  hole and an axle hole
1—2 x 6 plate
4—Technic pins
1—Technic axle, 5 studs long

BLACK BRICKS
2—Technic axles, 4 studs long
2—Technic axles, 6 studs long
2—Technic pins with friction ridges
  lengthwise and center slots

ASSORTED BRICKS
2—dark tan 16 x 16 plates
3—tan Technic axle pins
2—red Technic bushes
Various brown bricks, 2 studs wide
Various dark gray bricks and plates
Plants and trees

OTHER ITEMS
M-motor
AAA battery box

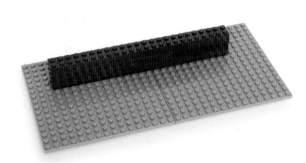

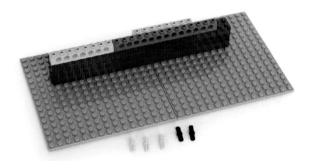

STEP 1: Start with two 16 x 16 plates, or use a 32 x 32 baseplate. Build a wall three bricks high. Make it 2 studs wide and 24 studs long. Use brown bricks, or substitute any other color.

STEP 2: Place two 1 x 8 light gray Technic bricks and a 1 x 14 dark gray Technic brick on the frame as shown. If you don't have these exact bricks, substitute smaller bricks to get the same total length. Find three tan axle pins and two black pins.

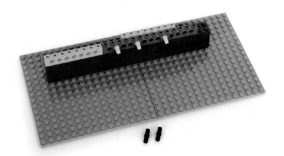

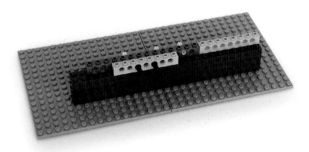

STEP 3: Insert the tan pins into the 1 x 14 dark gray Technic brick as shown.

STEP 4: Turn the base around and insert the black pins.

STEP 5: Find three 24-tooth gears, two 40-tooth gears, one 8-tooth gear, two axles (6 studs long) and one axle (4 studs long).

STEP 6: Attach the 24-tooth gears to the tan axle pins. Slide an axle (6 studs long) through each 40-tooth gear, and then slide the axle through the Technic bricks. Slide the 8-tooth gear onto an axle (4 studs long).

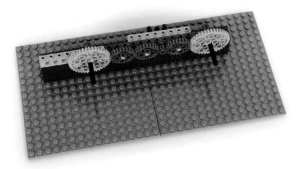

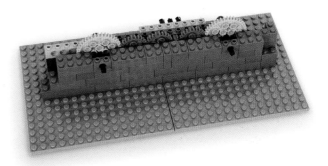

STEP 7: Slide a red Technic bush onto each axle (6 studs long) on the other side of the Technic bricks. This will hold them secure. Insert the axle (4 studs long) and the 8-tooth gear in between the 24-tooth gears.

STEP 8: Build a layer of dark gray bricks in front of the mechanism to hide it. Slide a 1 x 2 dark gray Technic brick over the two axles that stick out.

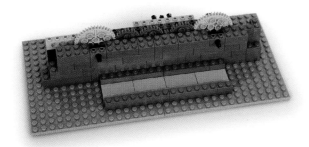

STEP 9: Build a path of tiles for the knights' platforms on which to slide back and forth. Use four 2 x 4 tiles, two 1 x 6 tiles and a 1 x 4 tile. Then put a row of bricks on either side.

STEP 10: Gather the bricks shown for building the platforms for the knights.

STEP 11: Slide #1 connectors onto each end of the two axles. Place a 1 x 2 dark gray brick next to a 1 x 2 dark gray Technic brick. Attach them with a 2 x 2 light gray plate. Make two of these.

STEP 12: Use the four light gray pins to connect the 1 x 2 liftarms and the platforms to the axles.

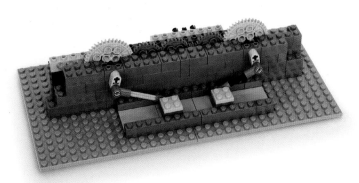

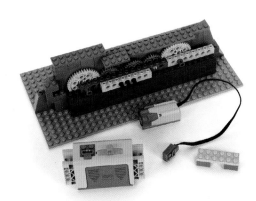

STEP 13: Slide the 1 x 2 liftarms onto the ends of the black axles. Your knight duel is almost ready for operation!

STEP 14: Turn the knight duel around to the back. Attach two 2 x 2 dark gray bricks to a 2 x 6 light gray plate. This will keep the cord out of the way.

STEP 15: Attach the motor to the black axle and two black pins. Then connect the motor to the battery box.

STEP 16: Use dark gray slope bricks and plates to make the front of the knight duel look like the side of a mountain, then add trees and plants. Find some knights and your dueling station is ready for action! Which knight will come out on top?

GENIUS LEGO INVENTIONS WITH BRICKS YOU ALREADY HAVE

DEEP FOREST TREASURE CAVE

Build a hidden cave that is full of gold, jewels and ancient weapons. Then pretend that your minifigure adventurers are following a treasure map that will lead them right to the treasure. There's just one problem: how does one get inside the cave? This cave is designed with a neat trick. Turn a knob at the top of the cave, and the hidden door mysteriously slides open!

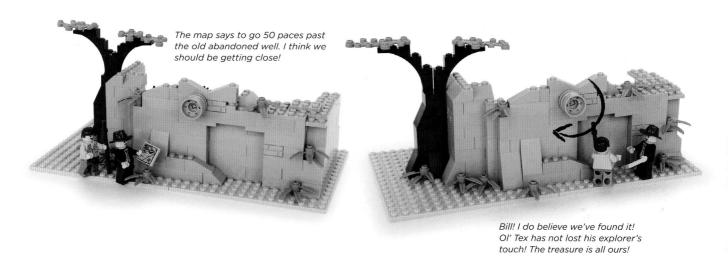

The map says to go 50 paces past the old abandoned well. I think we should be getting close!

Bill! I do believe we've found it! Ol' Tex has not lost his explorer's touch! The treasure is all ours!

Here it is! This must be the entrance! Now the map says, "At the hidden entrance to the cave, sing 'Happy Birthday' backward while patting your head and rubbing your belly. Then clap seven times and the door will open . . . ."

HOW IT WORKS

A gear and gear rack is the perfect mechanism for building a sliding door. First construct a door panel with bricks, and then build a track made of tiles for the door to slide on. Gear racks at the top of the door panel connect with a bevel gear at the top of the cave wall. Turn the bevel gear and it will slide the door open and closed. Super cool!

PARTS LIST

CAVE
2—16 x 16 tan plates
Various light gray bricks and plates
Light gray slope bricks
Brown bricks and slopes for creating
a tree

Leaves and plants
Treasure—swords, jewels, coins, etc.

MECHANISM
1—black Technic bevel gear, 20 tooth
2—1 x 4 black Technic gear racks

3—1 x 4 light gray tiles
1—wheel with an axle hole
1—1 x 2 light gray Technic brick
1—Technic axle, 3 studs long

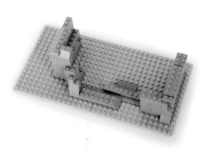

STEP 1: Build a cave with three sides. At the front, build a track for the door to slide on. Use four 1 x 4 light gray tiles. The track will need to have some bricks on either side to keep the door from falling over.

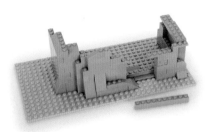

STEP 2: Keep adding bricks to the front of the cave. Leave a six-stud opening for the door and use a long light gray brick to span the top of the doorway.

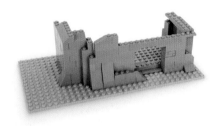

STEP 3: Complete the door opening. Add slope bricks around the base of the cave to give it a more rocky and natural look.

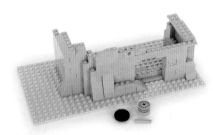

STEP 4: Place a 1 x 2 light gray Technic brick at the top of the cave just to the left of the door opening. Then find a 20-tooth bevel gear, an axle (3 studs long) and a wheel with an axle hole.

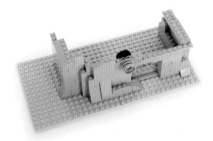

STEP 5: Slide the axle through the Technic brick and attach the gear and the wheel to either side.

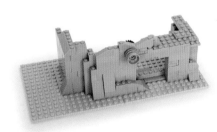

STEP 6: Hide the gear by adding more light gray bricks and slopes to the top of the cave.

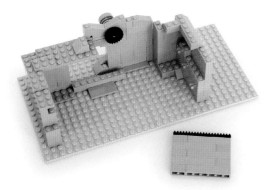

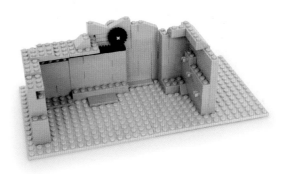

STEP 7: Stack light gray bricks to make a door that is 8 studs wide. Build five layers, then place two 1 x 4 gear racks on top.

STEP 8: Place the door on top of the tile track and under the gear.

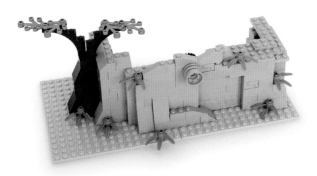

STEP 9: Make the cave look like it's in the middle of a forest by adding a tree and plants. Build the tree with brown bricks and slope bricks. Add tree branch bricks if you have them.

STEP 10: Fill the inside of the cave with treasure! Use 1 x 2 light gray bricks with a clip on the side to display swords and spears on the walls. Fill a brown treasure chest with coins and jewels. Your minifigures will be thrilled to discover this treasure stash!

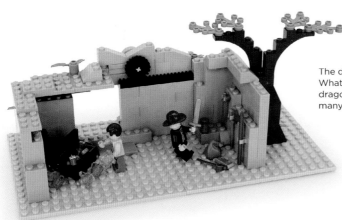

The door should slide open easily when you turn the light gray wheel. What a fun secret cave! Another fun idea is to make the cave a dragon's lair or a hideout for Old West cowboys. There are so many possibilities!

PROFESSOR FIDDLE-STICKS' CRAZY CAR

Build a totally wacky, crazy car that bumps up and down as you drive it along. It looks like the perfect vehicle for a slightly absentminded professor who is more concerned with his newest invention than following the latest styles! Once you have completed the car, you'll want to create Professor Fiddlesticks' Wacky Tree House (page 168) as well.

HOW IT WORKS

A wheel may be one of the simplest machines there is, but can you imagine trying to live life without it? Your car certainly wouldn't move very fast if you had to drag it down the road, and let's not even think about having to walk everywhere instead of hopping on your bike!

Wheeled vehicles need axles for the wheels to be able to turn. Picture what would happen if your car's wheels were just bolted to the sides of the car. It wouldn't go anywhere, would it? Wheels need to be able to turn around an axle for a car to go places. In this car, however, the wheel is fixed in position relative to the axle. The wheels can still turn, because the axle can spin freely inside the holes in the Technic bricks.

Now the twist to this car is that the axle is inserted in the wheels (the 40-tooth gears) in an off-center position. This causes the entire back of the car to raise and lower as you push it—pretty crazy!

PARTS LIST

YELLOW BRICKS
1—4 x 8 plate
2—2 x 4 plates
1—1 x 6 plate
2—1 x 4 plates
2—1 x 3 bricks
2—1 x 2 bricks
4—2 x 2 slopes
2—2 x 4 x 1⅓ bricks, modified with a curved top
2—1 x 1 round plates
1—chair

MEDIUM AZURE BRICKS
1—2 x 4 brick
1—2 x 4 plate
1—1 x 6 plate
2—2 x 2 inverted slopes

WHITE BRICKS
1—1 x 2—2 x 2 bracket
1—1 x 2—1 x 4 bracket
2—2 x 2 dishes
1—1 x 4 tile
1—steering wheel

ASSORTED BRICKS
1—6 x 12 light green plate
2—1 x 2 light gray Technic bricks
2—1 x 4 light gray Technic bricks

2—Technic gears, 40 tooth
2—2 x 4 x 1⅓ red bricks, modified with a curved top
2—1 x 3 red plates
4—1 x 2 purple bricks
2—1 x 8 black Technic bricks
1—black Technic axle, 10 studs long
1—black axle, 8 studs long
1—2 x 6 windshield
4—1 x 1 translucent orange cones
4—flames
2—wheels with axle holes
1—1 x 4 silver plate with angled tubes

OTHER ITEMS
2—rubber bands

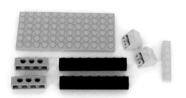

STEP 1: Gather the bricks shown for building the base of the car.

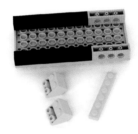

STEP 2: Attach the four Technic bricks to the underside of the 6 x 12 plate.

STEP 3: Attach the two inverted slopes to the underside at the front of the car. Then add the 1 x 6 plate.

STEP 4: Turn the car over and place two 2 x 4 x 1⅓ bricks with a curved top on the front of the car. Then find the bricks shown.

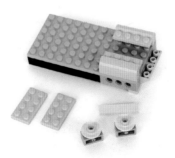

STEP 5: Build silly headlights by attaching 1 x 1 yellow round plates to 2 x 2 white dishes. Attach these to the holes in two 1 x 2 Technic bricks.

STEP 6: Attach the headlights and yellow plates to the front of the car as shown.

STEP 7: Add a 2 x 4 medium azure brick and two 2 x 2 yellow slopes. Then gather the bricks shown.

STEP 8: Place the 2 x 4 medium azure plate on top of the brick of the same color. Add a 1 x 4 yellow plate and a steering wheel.

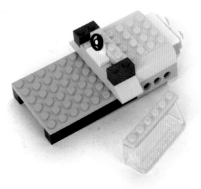

STEP 9: Add another 1 x 4 yellow plate on top of the first. Then attach a 1 x 2 purple brick on each side of the car. Attach the 1 x 6 yellow plate to the windshield.

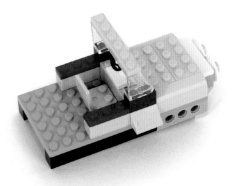

STEP 10: Attach the windshield to the car. Then add a chair. Place a 1 x 3 yellow brick and a 1 x 3 red plate on each side.

STEP 11: Add a 2 x 2 yellow slope, a 1 x 2 purple brick and a 1 x 2 yellow brick to each side. Then gather the bricks shown.

STEP 12: Assemble the roof of the car as shown and add a 1 x 2—2 x 2 white bracket to the back of the car.

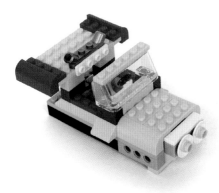

STEP 13: Attach the crazy-looking roof to the car.

STEP 14: Find an axle (8 studs long), an axle (10 studs long), two 40-tooth gears, two wheels with X-shaped axle holes and four flames with 1 x 1 translucent orange cones. Find two rubber bands that will fit snugly on the 40-tooth gears.

STEP 15: Put on the front wheels using the axle (10 studs long).

STEP 16: Slide the smaller axle (8 studs long) through the second to last holes in the Technic bricks and add the 40-tooth gears. Make sure to place both gears on corresponding holes.

STEP 17: Put a rubber band on each gear to give it enough friction that it will roll well. Without the rubber bands, the gears will slide on a table rather than roll. Then attach the flames and the car is complete. Just imagine, this crazy car is rocket powered—ha!

Now pretend that Professor Fiddlesticks is heading off to an inventing convention in his crazy car. Or maybe he's picking up some plutonium for powering his next gadget.

PROFESSOR FIDDLE-STICKS' WACKY TREE HOUSE

Wouldn't it be awesome to have a house in a tree? Build Professor Fiddlesticks a totally wacky tree house with a tiny furnished kitchen, a tiny bed and even a tiny porch. Of course, he needs a way to get up to his tree house, and an inventor like Professor Fiddlesticks will think of just the thing—an elevator with a clever pulley system. He can park his Crazy Car (page 164) under his tree and then ride the elevator right up to the door. You can lock the elevator in place at the top by attaching a 1 x 4 brick to the winding mechanism. It will hold down the bars on the brown wheel to keep it from turning.

HOW IT WORKS

Professor Fiddlesticks' elevator is operated by a simple pulley. Unlike the Powerful Pulleys (page 121), this pulley does not increase the lifting power. However, even though there is no mechanical advantage, it is still easier to lift something using a pulley because pulling down is easier than lifting something off the ground. If you have a tree house or a play fort in your yard or a set of stairs inside, you can build your own pulley system! You can purchase an inexpensive pulley at the hardware store, or you can simply run a piece of rope over a tree branch or the stair railing. Attach a bucket to your rope. You can lift things in your bucket by pulling on the free end of the rope!

PARTS LIST

TREE

1—16 x 16 bright green plate
Various brown bricks and slopes
1 x 3 and 1 x 4 plates to use as tree branches
2—4 x 6 brown plates
Tree leaves

HOUSE

2—6 x 10 light gray plates
1—6 x 6 light gray plate
1—4 x 6 light gray plate
1—2 x 6 light gray plate
1—8 x 16 light blue plate (or substitute another color)
2—doors
3—1 x 4 x 2 white picket fences
4—1 x 4 x 3 windows
3—1 x 4 x 3 clear panels
2—2 x 3 brown plates
1—2 x 4 brown plate
4—2 x 2 lime green inverted slopes
Various lime green bricks and plates
Various yellow bricks and plates
2 x 2, 2 x 4 and 2 x 2 corner dark blue slope bricks for the roof

SINK, BED AND TABLE

1—1 x 4 light gray brick
1—2 x 4 light gray brick
2—light gray faucet/nozzle
2—1 x 2 x 1 light gray panels
4—1 x 1 light gray corner panels
1—1 x 4 tan plate
2—2 x 4 tan plates
1—4 x 4 tan plate
1—4 x 4 blue plate
2—2 x 4 white plates
4—1 x 1 brown round plates
1—4 x 4 brown plate
1—2 x 2 brown round brick
2—chairs
1—1 x 1 light gray round brick
Flowers

PULLEY MECHANISM

1—4 x 4 bright green plate
1—4 x 6 dark gray plate
1—1 x 2 light gray Technic brick
2—1 x 2 dark gray Technic bricks
1—wheel with a pin hole
2—1 x 2 lime green plates
1—1 x 4 lime green brick
1—4 x 6 lime green plate

4—1 x 2 light gray bricks, two bricks high
4—1 x 2 light gray bricks
1—4 x 6 yellow plate
1—2 x 2 black round tile with lifting ring
1—Technic axle, 7 studs long
1—6 x 6 light gray plate
1—brown Technic axle connector hub with four bars
6—2 x 4 dark azure bricks
4—1 x 2 dark azure bricks

OTHER ITEMS

String

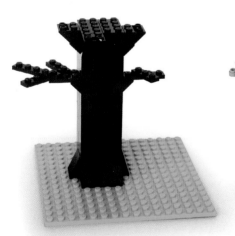

STEP 1: Build a tree for the tree house. Use brown bricks to build a tree trunk shape in whatever size you want.

STEP 2: Place two 4 x 6 plates on top of the tree to make a nice flat surface for attaching the house. Add leaves.

STEP 3: Set the tree trunk aside and build the house. Gather the plates shown.

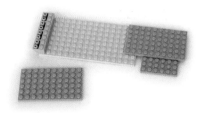  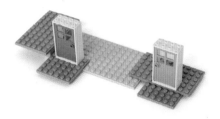

STEP 4: Attach the plates as shown and add a row of 2 x 2 inverted slopes to the left side.

STEP 5: Place the final 6 x 10 plate on the row of inverted slopes.

STEP 6: Attach a 4 x 6 plate and a 2 x 6 plate (or a 6 x 6 plate) to make the porch, then add two doors.

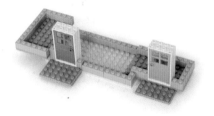  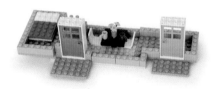

STEP 7: Build a row of lime green bricks around the perimeter of the house.

STEP 8: It's easier to add furniture before building all the walls. Make a sink out of bricks and panels, then create a tiny minifigure-size bed.

STEP 9: Build a little kitchen table with a 2 x 2 round brick and a 4 x 4 plate. A 1 x 1 round brick makes a nice vase for flowers.

STEP 10: Complete the walls and add windows. Use any colors and get creative with the types of windows you have.

STEP 11: Add slope bricks as roof tiles. Build a window box for flowers by attaching two 2 x 3 brown plates to the wall as you are building. Place a 2 x 4 plate under the 2 x 3 plates for extra strength. Add fence bricks to the porch.

STEP 12: Add a 1 x 4 lime green brick just over the front door. Gather the bricks shown for building the pulley elevator.

STEP 13: Use the gray pin to attach the wheel to the 1 x 2 Technic brick. Stack the two 1 x 2 lime green plates and put them on top of the Technic brick. Then attach the 4 x 6 plate and connect this to the 1 x 4 lime green brick on the house.

STEP 14: Build the little elevator car for Professor Fiddlesticks to ride in. Tie a piece of string to a 2 x 2 tile with a ring on top.

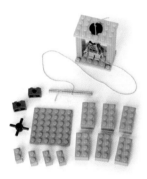

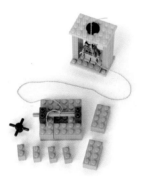

STEP 15: With a few more bricks, you can build a mechanism to wind up the string. It will also hold the elevator in place at the top. Tie the other end of the string to an axle (7 studs long).

STEP 16: Attach four 2 x 4 bricks to the 6 x 6 plate. Then add two 1 x 2 Technic bricks and slide the axle into the holes.

STEP 17: Add the rest of the bricks. Slide the brown brick with knobs onto the axle so that you can turn the axle. It's called a Technic axle connector hub with four bars.

STEP 18: Attach the winding mechanism to the 16 x 16 plate. Thread the string through the groove in the wheel, and your elevator is ready to go! Turn the brown wheel to wind up the string, and then lock it in place by attaching a 1 x 4 brick.

If you prefer to just pull the string with your hand, you can skip the winding mechanism. It's totally up to you!

Wow, what a cozy and adorable house! It's the perfect place to come home to after a long day of inventing.

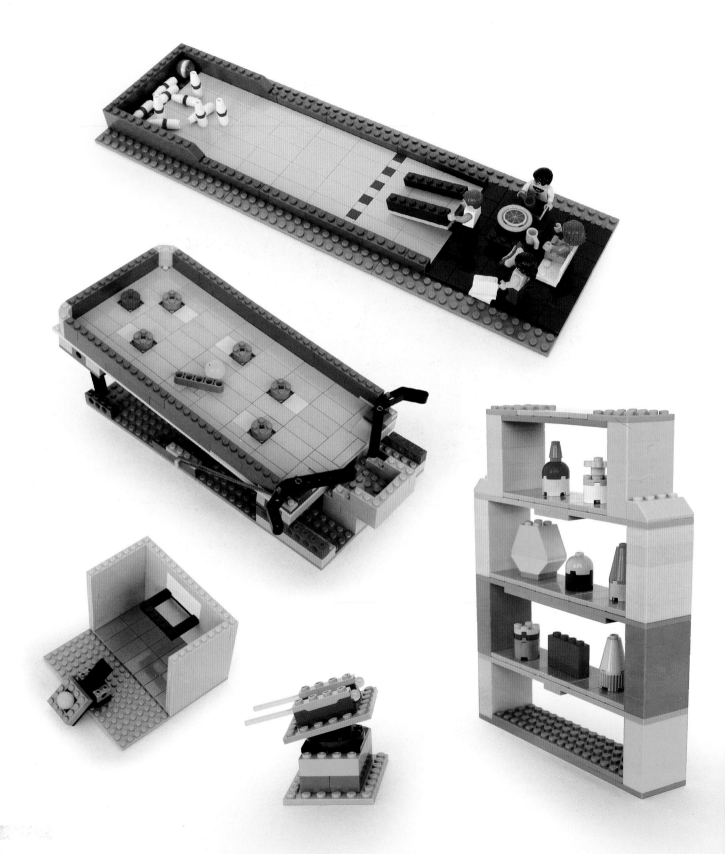

CONSTRUCT AND COMPETE BUILDABLE GAMES

You might not think to connect science and sports, but where there's motion, there's a physics concept involved! Use your LEGO bricks to build some super fun game challenges. You'll be exploring principles of motion while constructing games that you can either play on your own or with a friend. Learn about the concept of trajectories by building a basketball hoop with a mini catapult that launches the ball. Then create your own three-level marble maze and see if a friend or family member can solve it by rolling the ball along the correct path. Turn your bricks into a working pinball game, a bowling alley and more!

SUPER HOOPS
BASKETBALL GAME

Build a basketball hoop shooting challenge! Construct a simple catapult that launches the ball. Can you hit the catapult with just enough force to get the ball through the hoop? Try playing a game against a friend. Take turns making shots and see who can score 10 baskets fastest! Or build a second one so you can compete at the same time to see who can score a basket first.

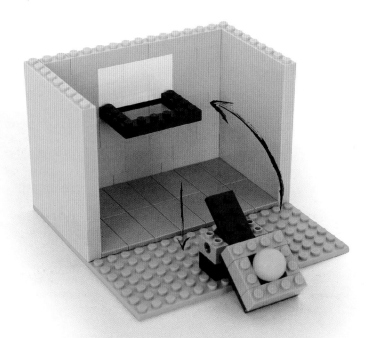

HOW IT WORKS

You might not realize this, but a catapult is actually a first-class lever. An object that is launched into the air is called a projectile. In this game, the projectile is the ball that is launched by the catapult. Any projectile follows a curved path through the air called its trajectory. The shape of the curve, however, depends on a few factors. Can you guess what they are? The angle at which the projectile is released plays a big part. Think about throwing a ball straight out in front of you versus throwing a ball straight up into the air. The ball would not follow the same path in those two situations, would it? Speed is also a factor in an object's trajectory, as well as gravity. As a ball is traveling through the air, gravity is working to eventually bring it down. A ball launched with greater speed will travel farther than a ball (of the same mass) launched with less speed. If you're trying to hit a particular target, such as a hoop, the distance of the projectile from the target is also an important factor.

In this LEGO basketball game, the ball will be released at the same angle each time. You can experiment with the factors of the force you use to hit the catapult and the distance that the catapult is located away from the basket. As you play, observe and figure out the best way to get a perfect shot.

PARTS LIST

BROWN BRICKS
7—1 x 4 plates
1—1 x 2 plate
1—4 x 4 plate
1—2 x 6 plate
2—1 x 2 bricks

WHITE BRICKS
2—1 x 4 plates
2—1 x 2 plates
2—1 x 4 bricks
2—1 x 2 bricks

LIGHT GRAY BRICKS
2—1 x 2 Technic bricks
2—1 x 2 bricks
2—1 x 4 bricks
14—2 x 4 gray tiles

ASSORTED BRICKS
1—16 x 16 bright green plate
1—2 x 2 dark gray brick with two pins
Various tan bricks for building the basketball court walls, or substitute any color

OTHER ITEMS
1—plastic LEGO ball

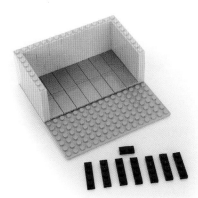

STEP 1: Grab a 16 x 16 plate and build the basketball court. Use fourteen 2 x 4 tiles to make the floor. Then build a three-sided wall that is five bricks tall. The game is more fun with a tile surface so that the ball can roll, but it will work without the tiles. Gather the plate bricks shown.

STEP 2: Begin the hoop by attaching three 1 x 4 brown plates to the wall of the court as shown. Then connect a 1 x 4 plate and a 1 x 2 plate by attaching another 1 x 4 plate on top.

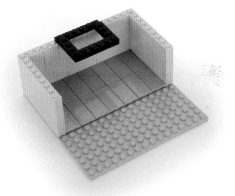

STEP 3: Place another 1 x 4 brown plate on each side of the hoop. Then add the plates you connected in the previous step to the front of the hoop.

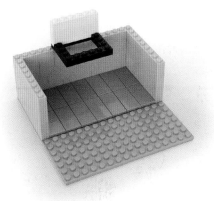

STEP 4: Build the backboard using two 1 x 4 white plates, two 1 x 2 white plates, two 1 x 4 bricks and two 1 x 2 bricks.

STEP 5: Complete the court walls by adding four more layers of tan bricks.

STEP 6: Gather the bricks shown for building the catapult.

STEP 7: Attach the light gray bricks to the perimeter of the 4 x 4 brown plate. Place each 1 x 2 Technic brick on top of a 1 x 2 brown brick.

STEP 8: Connect each Technic brick to one side of the 2 x 2 dark gray brick with two pins. Then attach the basket to the 2 x 6 plate so that it overlaps by two rows of studs.

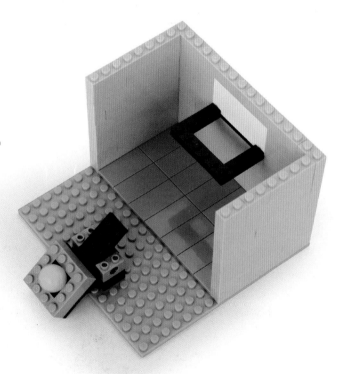

STEP 9: Attach the catapult to the 16 x 16 base, and then find a plastic LEGO ball. It's game time! Be sure to be safe! If you don't have a plastic LEGO ball, use something lightweight for your ball rather than shooting a heavy marble.

3-D MARBLE MAZE CUBE

This multilevel marble maze is especially fun to build because you can design it any way you like! Insert a ball in the opening on top. The floor on each level is built with a hole in one corner so that the ball can drop down to the next level, but it's a little tricky because you can't completely see inside! Solve the maze by tilting the cube and navigating the ball through all three levels and then out the door on the bottom. Tinker with your maze until you get it just right, and then challenge your friends to solve it!

HOW IT WORKS

When you design the layout for your marble maze, you'll be putting your math skills to good use. Experiment with where you put the hole for the ball to drop to the next level. What location for the hole would be the easiest to find with the ball? What would be the hardest? You can try putting the holes in the corners or make it super tricky and put one somewhere in the center. Just make sure that you have an open path below the hole and not a wall!

PARTS LIST

ASSORTED BRICKS
2—16 x 16 plates
12—1 x 4 x 3 clear panels
Various gray or light gray plates
Bricks 1 stud wide

OTHER ITEMS
1—plastic LEGO ball or marble

BUILDING TIPS

If you use a plastic LEGO ball, you'll need to make sure that the path is at least 3 studs wide in all places, including turns. You'll want to plan each level by building one layer of bricks and making sure it works before completing all the walls.

If you don't have the clear panels shown, substitute with windows of any type. It's fun if you can see into the maze a little, but not so much that the maze becomes too easy to solve!

STEP 1: Start with the bottom floor of the maze and work your way up. Choose a spot for the ball to exit the maze and leave it open. Each layer is three bricks high.

STEP 2: To build the second layer, cover the first layer with plates except for an opening where the ball can drop down. Then construct the walls.

STEP 3: Build the top layer by again adding a layer of plates and leaving an opening for the ball. Because this layer is the top, leave an opening for inserting the ball.

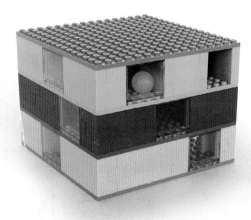

STEP 4: Complete your 3-D marble maze cube by attaching a second 16 x 16 plate on top. Then you're ready to play or to challenge your friends!

If you have enough bricks, you might want to add another layer to make your maze extra hard to solve.

TARGET PRACTICE BRICK TOWER

Turn your spring shooter missiles into a super cool target practice game! Build a tower with shelves covered with tiles. Then create fun targets from all kinds of bricks. Create a base for the spring shooter bricks that tilts and rotates so that you can carefully aim your missiles for just the right shot. Once you have built the game, see if you can develop your skill and knock down every target!

HOW IT WORKS

Just like the Super Hoops Basketball Game (page 174), this game uses a projectile traveling on a trajectory in order to score a point. Unlike the basketball game, however, you'll need to change the angle of your missile's launch in order to knock down all the targets. With a little practice, you should be able to develop some great aiming skills. How many tries will it take you to knock down every target?

The spring shooter bricks harness potential energy to create motion. When you insert a missile into the brick, the missile compresses a spring. The compressed spring now has potential energy. A little notch on the missile catches on the brick and holds it in place. When you push down on the missile, it releases the spring, making it free to move again. Potential energy is converted to kinetic energy, and the missile shoots forward with impressive force!

PARTS LIST

FRAME
Various plates in any color
38—2 x 4 bricks
4—2 x 2 slopes
26—2 x 4 tiles

SPRING SHOOTER BASE
1—6 x 8 lime green plate
1—6 x 6 light gray plate
1—4 x 4 turntable base
1—4 x 4 dark gray round plate
2—2 x 6 blue bricks
3—2 x 4 dark azure bricks
1—2 x 2 hinge plate with base
2—spring shooter bricks with missiles

TARGETS
2 x 2 round bricks
2 x 2 cones
2 x 2 domes
Slope bricks
Get creative with any bricks in any color!

STEP 1: Build a frame for your game. Use overlapping plates to build the shelves. The tiles on top of the plates are important for reducing friction between the targets and the shelf so that they are easy to knock off. If you don't have enough tiles, try placing tiles only where the targets will sit, with studs exposed between tiles.

STEP 2: Now create some targets to hit! A wide target, such as the stack of 1 x 4 bricks, is the easiest to hit. Small round targets are more challenging. Get creative with your targets and use whatever bricks and colors you like.

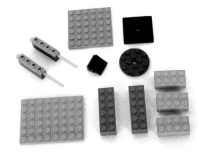

STEP 3: Gather the bricks shown for building the base that will hold the spring shooter bricks.

STEP 4: Place two 2 x 6 bricks on the 6 x 8 plate. Then add three 2 x 4 bricks.

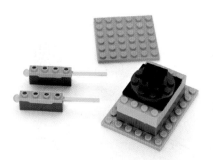

STEP 5: Attach the turntable base with the 4 x 4 round plate attached. Then add the 2 x 2 hinge with base.

STEP 6: To complete the target, attach a 6 x 6 light gray plate to the 2 x 2 hinge. Then attach your spring shooter bricks. The base will rotate in a circle, and the hinge allows it to tilt.

Now line up your targets and take aim! Challenge a friend to try it too.

EPIC PINBALL

Use your LEGO bricks to create a working pinball game! This game is a simplified version of the real thing, but the goal is the same. Use the flippers to propel the ball up the table and score as many points as possible before the ball drops down the drain. Keep score by counting how many times the ball hits the blue bricks. Count the red brick as a bonus score. You can decide how many points each brick is worth. Another option is to keep score by timing how long you can keep the ball on the table before it rolls into the drain.

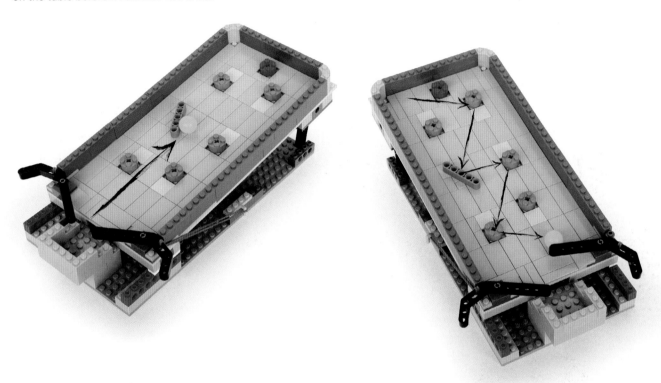

HOW IT WORKS

The tilt of the pinball machine means that gravity is your enemy in this game! The ball will naturally roll down the table and toward the drain, so you'll have to act quickly to keep it from falling. This type of response is called "hand-eye coordination." Scientists use this term to describe any situation in which a person relies on visual information to make decisions about what the hands need to do. You do this when you are writing. Your eyes watch your hand forming the letters, and your brain uses the information from your eyes to help your hand make adjustments to keep the writing neat. Hand-eye coordination is also important for hitting a baseball with a bat or putting a coin in the slot of a gumball machine. Success at this pinball game depends on your reaction time, or how quickly your muscles react when your eyes see the ball rolling toward the drain. Does your reaction time improve after more practice playing the game?

The rubber bands provide some resistance to the flippers and make it easier to give the ball a good solid smack. They restrict the movement of the paddles somewhat, making the paddles easier to control.

PARTS LIST

LIGHT GRAY BRICKS
2—2 x 8 bricks
5—1 x 6 bricks
6—2 x 4 bricks
2—1 x 4 plates with an arm down
38—2 x 4 tiles
9—1 x 4 tiles
4—1 x 3 tiles
7—1 x 2 tiles
2—1 x 1 tiles
2—2 x 2 curved slopes
4—2 x 2 rounded corner bricks
2—1 x 4 plates
2—1 x 8 plates
2—2 x 6 bricks
3—1 x 4 bricks
1—6 x 6 plate
2—1 x 3 bricks

DARK GRAY BRICKS
2—1 x 4 Technic bricks
4—1 x 2 Technic bricks
2—1 x 4 plates
2—1 x 6 plates
2—1 x 6 bricks
2—2 x 2 bricks modified with a top
  pin and 1 x 2 side plates
7—1 x 4 bricks
11—1 x 6 bricks
3—1 x 8 bricks
1—1 x 2 brick
2—1 x 8 plates
2—1 x 6 plates

DARK TAN BRICKS
2—16 x 16 dark tan plates
1—6 x 6 dark tan plate
1—2 x 6 dark tan plate

ASSORTED BRICKS
2—16 x 16 tan plates
2—1 x 8 red Technic bricks
2—1 x 3 black Technic liftarms
2—1 x 7 black Technic liftarms
8—black Technic pins
5—2 x 2 yellow tiles
5—2 x 2 blue round bricks
1—2 x 2 red round brick
1—1 x 5 blue Technic liftarm
1—2 x 2 dark azure tile with one stud
  on top
2—1 x 11½ black Technic liftarms,
  double bent

OTHER ITEMS
2—rubber bands

STEP 1: Attach two 16 x 16 plates with a 6 x 6 plate and a 2 x 6 plate.

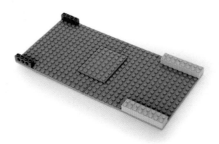

STEP 2: Add two 2 x 8 bricks and two 1 x 4 Technic bricks.

STEP 3: Place two 1 x 8 red Technic bricks on top of the light gray bricks. Then attach a 1 x 3 liftarm to each one by using a black pin. Attach a black pin to the top hole on each liftarm as well. Then add two 1 x 7 black liftarms on the other end of the game. Attach them with a black pin and insert an additional black pin at the top of each one.

STEP 4: Build two supports. Attach two 1 x 6 light gray bricks and a 1 x 2 dark gray Technic brick to a 1 x 4 dark gray plate. Then make a second one.

STEP 5: Build two more supports. This time, attach two 2 x 4 light gray bricks and a 1 x 2 dark gray Technic brick to a 1 x 6 dark gray plate.

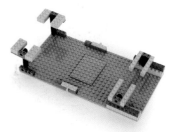

STEP 6: Attach the supports to the liftarms using the black pins. On each side of the base, add a 1 x 6 dark gray brick and a 1 x 4 light gray plate with an arm down.

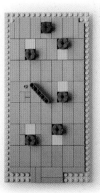

STEP 7: Use two 16 x 16 plates to build the table and cover them with tiles. Use the 2 x 2 round bricks as bumpers. You can also attach liftarms to 2 x 2 tiles with one stud on top to create ramps.

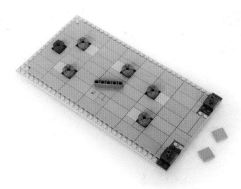

STEP 8: Place two 2 x 2 bricks with a pin on top on both bottom corners of the game.

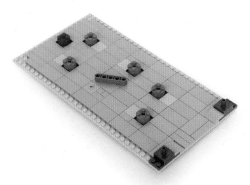

STEP 9: Attach two 2 x 2 curved slopes to secure the bricks with pins in place.

STEP 10: Place a 1 x 8 light gray plate on each side of the game. Then add two rows of dark gray bricks. Use the 2 x 2 rounded corner bricks in the corners. Gather the bricks shown.

STEP 11: Attach a 1 x 4 plate on each bottom corner, and then add a 1 x 6 plate on each side. Overlapping bricks will keep the bricks with pins from coming off under the pressure of the rubber bands and liftarms.

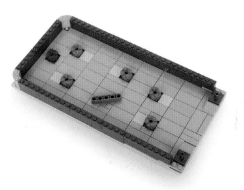

STEP 12: Complete each side with two 1 x 4 bricks and then a 1 x 8 plate on top.

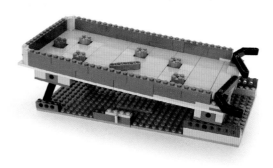

STEP 13: Grab two liftarms and attach them to the pins. These are 1 x 11½ (double bent).

STEP 14: Attach the game table to the supports. You can adjust the supports to create just the right angle.

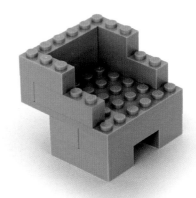

STEP 15: Attach a rubber band to each liftarm using a loop knot. You may want to remove them from the table to make this easier.

STEP 16: Build a drain to catch the ball when it rolls down the table. Use a 6 x 6 plate. Put two 2 x 6 bricks and two 2 x 4 bricks underneath. Then build walls on the top of the 6 x 6 plate using three 1 x 4 bricks, a 1 x 6 brick and two 1 x 3 bricks.

STEP 17: Stretch the rubber bands around the arms on the base. Then you're ready to play!

To play, move the flippers and hit the ball back up the table. Count how many bumpers you can hit before it finally falls down into the drain!

MINIFIGURE BOWLING ALLEY

Create a bowling game complete with a bowling lane, pins and a ball! It's hard to aim on this tiny scale, so build a ramp to roll the ball down. Play the game yourself or challenge a friend to see who can get the higher score. Your minifigures will have a blast bowling too—and don't forget the pizza to make it an extra special event! When you complete the bowling alley, you might want to build an entire family entertainment center for minifigures by designing some arcade games or building a basketball game (page 174).

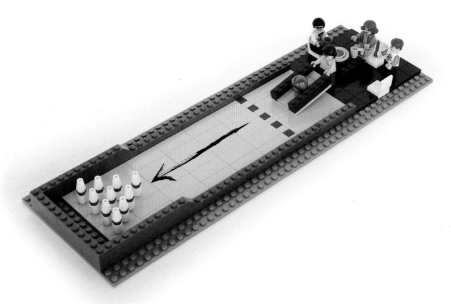

HOW IT WORKS

Bowling may look as simple as heaving a heavy ball onto a smooth lane, but there's more to it than that! Professional bowlers know that there is a LOT of physics involved in scoring the most possible strikes. The ball transfers energy to the pins. The greater the speed of the ball, the more energy it will transfer to the pins, and the more they will fly around! Experienced bowlers get their ball to spin so that it will hook a little as it hits the pins. The best place to make contact with the pins is the space between the first and third pins. This will cause the pins to ricochet in such a way that they all fall down! Or at least that's the hope.

It may be a little tough to get a marble to spin, but you can experiment with glass marbles versus steel ball bearings. You can experiment with the length of the ramp and with rolling the ball from your hand versus rolling it down the ramp. You can also move the ramp to change the angle at which the ball heads down the lane. What is the best way to roll the ball so that you score the most points?

PARTS LIST

DARK GRAY BRICKS
1—1 x 10 brick
1—1 x 8 brick
8—1 x 6 bricks
6—1 x 4 bricks
3—1 x 3 bricks
3—1 x 2 bricks
1—1 x 1 brick
2—1 x 2 slopes

BROWN BRICKS
2—1 x 4 bricks
2—1 x 2 bricks
1—4 x 4 plate
1—2 x 2 brick

ASSORTED BRICKS
3—16 x 16 dark tan plates
40—2 x 4 tan tiles
5—1 x 1 tan tiles
5—1 x 2 red tiles
31—2 x 2 dark blue tiles

4—chairs
2—2 x 2 white tiles with one stud on top
10—1 x 1 white round bricks
10—1 x 1 white cones
10—1 x 1 red round plates
1—4 x 6 tan plate
1—2 x 4 light gray tile
2—1 x 2 light gray tiles
1—2 x 2 hinge plate and base

OTHER ITEMS
1 or more marbles

DID YOU KNOW?

Most professional bowlers send the ball down the lane at about 19 miles (30.4 kilometers) per hour. It takes a lot of practice to bowl like that!

BUILDING TIP

If you don't have enough tiles to make the bowling lane, simply build the walls for the lane and set them on a table or countertop to create a flat surface for bowling. The great thing about this setup is that you can better experiment with the distance between the ramp and the pins. However you build it, you'll love this game!

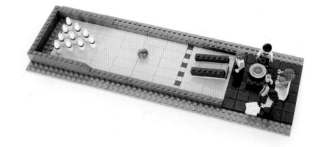

STEP 1: Build your bowling lane with three 16 x 16 plates as the base. If you don't have three of that size, use smaller plates to build the same area. The bowling lane has six rows with five 2 x 4 tiles in each row, then a row of 1 x 1 tan tiles and 1 x 1 red tiles, then two more rows of five 2 x 4 tiles. Build a row of bricks on each side of the lane and make this row two bricks high on all three sides at the end. This will keep the ball from going out of the lane.

STEP 2: Create a seating area with chairs and a table. The table is a 4 x 4 plate on top of a 2 x 2 brick. If you place the chairs on top of a 2 x 2 white tile with one stud on top, they will swivel. The chairs right next to each other won't swivel because they are so close together, but the other two will.

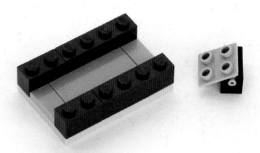

STEP 3: Build the pins by stacking a 1 x 1 white round brick, a 1 x 1 red round plate and a 1 x 1 white cone. There are 10 pins in the game.

STEP 4: Create a ramp with a 4 x 6 tan plate. Add brown bricks and some tiles for easy rolling. Then attach the ramp to a 2 x 2 hinge plate and base.

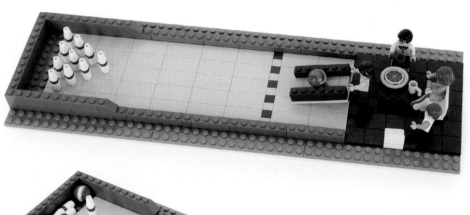

Now grab some marbles and give your game a try!

It's almost a strike! Well, sort of. Four pins are still standing. Remove the fallen pins and try for the spare!

ACKNOWLEDGMENTS

I am extremely grateful that I have so many people to thank who contributed their time and ideas to this book. Thank you to everyone at Page Street Publishing for making this an incredible book, and thank you to Sarah for being such an awesome editor. I really appreciate your ideas and encouragement and the fact that you take time to care about all the details.

Thank you to my oldest son Aidan for all your hard work on the mechanisms in this book. Aidan designed the construction crane, the dance floor, the scissor lift and the drummer, and we collaborated on many of the other designs such as the dog and the rubber band gun.

Thank you to my dad, Steve Packard, for contributing your engineering expertise to this book. Thanks for answering all my many phone calls about scientific concepts! Thank you also to Drew Irvin for checking the accuracy of the engineering concepts in this book. I really appreciate your input!

Thank you to Shawn Privett for creating ideas for this book and for being so enthusiastic about the project in general. Credit goes to Shawn for the clever mechanisms in the candy machine, the pinball game and the knight duel.

Thank you to Coolfolder on YouTube for allowing us to use your design for the marble spiral. It's a genius idea!

Thank you to Jason Allemann of JK Brickworks for allowing us to use a modification of your Trammel of Archimedes design in our dance floor. Such an incredible project!

Thank you to all of my readers at Frugal Fun for Boys and Girls, and readers of my books *Awesome LEGO Creations* and *Epic LEGO Adventures.* It's always a joy to hear which projects your kids love the best. I appreciate all of your enthusiastic support!

ABOUT THE AUTHOR

Sarah Dees is the creative mind behind the popular website Frugal Fun for Boys and Girls. She's the author of two other LEGO project books: *Awesome LEGO Creations with Bricks You Already Have* and *Epic LEGO Adventures with Bricks You Already Have*. She is an educator; wife to her wonderful husband, Jordan; and a busy mom of five LEGO-loving kids. She enjoys learning and exploring the outdoors with her kids, as well as creating all kinds of neat LEGO projects. It's not unusual for her playroom floor to be covered with LEGO bricks—with the entire family building! Her website is a fantastic resource for crafts, activities, STEM projects and games that children will love. Check out her latest projects, including LEGO ideas, at frugalfun4boys.com.

INDEX